# The Sons of the Gods and the Daughters of Men

**To Sibley Towner**

# The Sons of the Gods and the Daughters of Men

An Afro-Asiatic Interpretation of Genesis 1–11

Modupẹ Oduyọye



ORBIS BOOKS
Maryknoll, New York 10545

Second Printing, January 1987



---


Published in the United States of America by Orbis Books, Maryknoll, NY 10545
Published in Nigeria by Daystar Press, Ibadan

Manufactured in the United States of America

Manuscript editor: Lisa McGraw

---

**Library of Congress Cataloging in Publication Data**

Oduyọye, Modupẹ.
The sons of the gods and the daughters of men.

Includes bibliographical references and indexes.
1. Bible. O.T. Genesis I-XI—Criticism, interpretation, etc. I. Title.
BS1235.2.038 1983 222'.1106 83-6308
ISBN 0-88344-467-4 (pbk.)

---

Daystar ISBN 978-122-167-4

# Contents

# Maps

# Preface

This book is the substance of the Bible Studies that I led at the Clergy School of the Anglican Diocese of Ijẹbu in Odogbolu, Nigeria, during August 1979. The bishop, the Rt. Rev. I. B. O. Akintemi, left me free to choose my subject; and I chose the first eleven chapters of Genesis, which one might call the Scriptures to all human beings, since there is little specifically Jewish in the material and yet a lot that is Afro-Asiatic.

We had four sessions, so the compact nature of the corpus allowed us to begin on a subject and treat it in some detail. I chose not to begin "in the beginning"—at Genesis 1. Instead I began *in media res*—with the sons of the gods in Genesis 6. Who were these sons of the gods? Why does the Hebrew language have a word with a plural suffix as its word for "God" when Hebrew religion is antipolytheist? And thus I dug up the questions—those obvious in the English versions and those patent only to one who reads from the Hebrew text. The true nature of the literary corpus we were studying thus became clear, and the need for interpretation could not be questioned (see pp. 37–38). I then brought to bear on all the questions new light from Hamito-Semitic philology, showing up the prehistory of the text (see Introduction, below, and pp. 33–35).

The experience was revealing even for that audience of clergy who had long familiarity with the stories in English and in Yoruba. It was clearly new discovery, and they asked for books to study on the subject. Anxiety about what these unusual interpretations would do to the faith of the Christian *laos* was voiced by at least one person, an elderly clergyman. Christian preaching certainly needs a stronger pillar to lean upon than a basis of obscurantism.

On another occasion, at a conference on Science and the Christian Faith, at the Institute of Church and Society, Ibadan, during the discussion of a paper on the theory of evolution, another clergyman, this time a young lecturer, was alarmed that I should draw the attention of the conference to the Good News Bible version of Ecclesiastes 3:19–21 (see p. 84). Am I to believe that we are afraid to have some passages of the Bible examined closely?

I am completing this book at the Selly Oak Colleges, Birmingham, where I am teaching a Department of Mission course on Primal World-Views. We are spending some time examining these stories of what was believed to have happened "before Abraham was" so that Christians in environments of primal world-views may be equipped with the tools for recognizing those points of view which Jesus requires them to fulfill and not to abolish.

*MODUPẸ ODUYỌYE*

# Note on the Transcription of Words

## Semitic Words

| | | | | |
|---|---|---|---|---|
| *š* | is pronounced as | *sh* | in English | *shoe* |
| *č* | is pronounced as | *ch* | in English | *church* |
| *ṣ* | is pronounced as | *ts* | in English | *flotsam* |
| *ḥ* | is pronounced as | *ch* | in German | *hoch* |
| *ε* | is pronounced as | *e* | in English | *pen* |
| *iy* | is pronounced as | *ee* | in English | *bee* |
| *εy* | is lengthened *ε* | | | |
| *ay* | is a diphthong *(ai)* | | | |
| $o^w$ | is a long *o* | | | |
| $u^w$ | is a long *u* | | | |

## Yoruba and Other African Words

ṣ is the orthographical symbol for *sh* in English *shoe*

ọ is the orthographical symbol for *o* in English *pot*

ẹ is the orthographical symbol for *e* in English *pen*

Africa and the Middle East
Showing Principal Languages Cited

Equator
THE SOUTHERN AREA OF WIDER AFFINITY
". . . an ultimate level of external and internal [linguistic] unity which is clear and undisputable."
—David Dalby, *Language Map of Africa*

The Niger-Congo Language Area

# Introduction

There is a scheme to the material in Genesis 1–11:

*i.* The *to$^{w}$-l$^{e}$d-ot* ("genealogy") of the heavens and the earth when they were created (Gen. 2:4a)
*ii.* The book of the *to$^{w}$-l$^{e}$d-ot* of Adam (Gen. 5:1)
*iii.* The *to$^{w}$-l$^{e}$d-ot* of Noah (Gen. 6:9)
*iv.* The *to$^{w}$-l$^{e}$d-ot* of the sons of Noah (Gen. 10:1)

We are given a picture of false starts in Adam's progress—in the cultural and moral history of human beings. After Adam and *Ḥawwah* (Eve) preferred the knowledge that opens the eyes to the mystique of obedience to taboos that seem irrational, they were launched on the path of science. Of their two sons, *Qayin* (Cain) set out on the path of agriculture ("he was a worker of the soil") and urbanization ("he was a city builder," Gen. 4:17), giving birth to civilization (Yabal and Yubal) and technology (Tubal Qayin).

Twice the path led to violence and disaster: *Qayin* killed *Hɛbɛl* (Abel); and *Lamɛk* celebrated manslaughter with a song. That is, urbanization and civilization practically killed pastoral nomadism (*Hɛbɛl* was a shepherd), and the victor became a wanderer discovering how wide the world was and how peopled by unknown tribes.

After the disruptive violence of *Qayin,* Adam and *Ḥawwah* had to try again:

> And Adam knew his wife again
> And she gave birth to a son
> And he called his name *Šet* [Seth].

*Šet* was a replacement for *Hɛbɛl* whom *Qayin* had killed. *Šet* gave birth to Enosh, who, abandoning the disruptive path of science and technology, struck out on the path of religion. According to the Priestly scheme, it was Enosh who began the practice of invocation in the name of YHWH (Gen. 4:26b).

After the disastrous violence of *Lamɛk* and his progeny ("the earth was filled with *ḥamaṣ* [violence]," Gen. 6:13) came *Noaḥ* ("rest"). He built for the unknown future. But once more human beings tried to be like gods:

> Come, let us build ourselves a city, and a watchtower with its top in the skies, and let us make a name for ourselves lest we be scattered over the face of the earth [Gen. 11:4].

This trend began with *Qayin*, for he was a city builder. According to the scheme in Genesis 1–11, the civilization of Nok (*Qayin* called his city by the name of his son *Ḥanoʷk* [Enoch]) preceded the civilization of Babylon. Both, observed the Hebrew nomads, collapsed because the gods do not approve of such ambitious schemes to ensure permanent security.

Human beings must learn modesty in planning social institutions and designing technology. It was after World War I that someone said to his fellows: "Come, let us form the League of Nations that we may no longer suffer the scourge of war." After World War II, another person said: "Come, let us form the United Nations." And after the initial successes of decolonization in Africa, someone said: "Come, let us form the Organization of African Unity that our land may never more be expropriated." Another person sat down and devised Esperanto, hoping to teach all peoples one tongue. The story of the confusion of tongues at Babel shows what the Hebrews thought of the first international language, Akkadian. Some people are ever for building a tower of Babel "with its top in the skies." Reality, says Genesis 1–11, will always force them back to earth.

Why should one seek philological help from the Ewe language in southern Togo, West Africa, for solving problems in the Hebrew text of the Bible? One does not seek philological help at random: one looks for help from an area that on other occasions has proved helpful for similar problems. Thus the whole field of Semitic languages became a quarry for solving problems in Hebrew philology, and nobody now queries the procedure of seeking help from Ugaritic, Aramaic (northwest Semitic), Akkadian (northeast Semitic), Arabic (southeast Semitic), Ge'ez/Amharic (southwest Semitic).

The quarry was extended when Semitic languages were fixed in the wider family of Hamito-Semitic (Afro-Asiatic) languages: Semitic, Ancient Egyptian, Berber, Cushitic (in Ethiopia and the Horn of Africa), and Chadic (around Lake Chad in northeast Nigeria). This has now been carried beyond the province of debate: see, for example, J. H. Greenberg, *The Languages of Africa* (The Hague: Mouton & Co., 1969); J. Bynon & T. Bynon, eds., *Hamito-Semitica* (The Hague: Mouton & Co., 1974); C. T. Hodge, ed., *Afroasiatic—A Survey* (The Hague: Mouton, 1971); and I. M. Diakonoff, *The Semito-Hamitic Languages* (Moscow: Nauka, 1965).

The significance of this is:

(i) Semitic languages actually belong to a large family, four sections of which are entirely inside Africa. The Semitic languages of Ethiopia, the fifth section, number no less than ten.[1]

(ii) Hausa, the most widely spoken Nigerian language, the largest of the Chadic languages, is a Hamito-Semitic language (note: not a Semitic language) on an equal footing with Hebrew. The Hausa, be it noted, are totally black Africans; and the relationship of their language to the Semitic languages was worked out without a single piece of documentary, epigraphic, or archeological evidence. The sole incontrovertible evidence has been extrapolation from the comparative method—the inescapable facts being the evidence of the languages.

Thus far, I am reporting the present state of Hamito-Semitic studies, not my own original findings.

My own theory began with the study of Hebrew at Yale in 1964, study of comparative Semitic linguistics at the Linguistic Institute of the Linguistics Society of America on a grant from the American Council of Learned Societies in 1965, study of Arabic at Yale in 1965–66, and study of Middle Egyptian in London in 1969–70. With eighteen years of accumulation of data and testing of working hypotheses, I know where to prospect for gold: I do not seek philological light on the Hebrew of the Old Testament simply anywhere from Britain to Japan. I seek it *(i)* within the Hamito-Semitic family and *(ii)* within the wide scope of Niger-Congo languages of Africa from Senegal to Cape Town, between which and

"Hamitic" (Ancient Egyptian, Berber, Cushitic, and Chadic) J. H. Greenberg says there are signs of an "extremely remote relationship."[2] That relationship it has been my business to document (for comparative and historical linguistics) and to exploit (for philology, which includes Old Testament exegesis). An extremely remote relationship is no less a relationship: the remoteness is a matter of time span. My first book on this subject—*The Vocabulary of Yoruba Religious Discourse*—was published in 1972.

# 1

# The *to$^{w}$-l$^{e}$d-ot* of the Heavens and the Earth

Genesis 2:4 begins with the sentence:

*’ellɛh to$^{w}$-l$^{e}$d-ot haš-šamay-im w$^{e}$-ha-’arɛṣ b$^{e}$-hib-bar$^{e}$’-am*
*b$^{e}$-yo$^{w}$m ‘as-o$^{w}$t YHWH (’$^{\varepsilon}$loh-iym) ’ɛrɛṣ w$^{e}$-šamay-im. . . .*

These are the *to$^{w}$-l$^{e}$d-ot* of the heavens and the earth when they were caused to be created:
On the day Yahweh (whom the myths call gods) made earth and the heavens. . . .

Contrasted with the beginning of Genesis 5—

*zɛh sefɛr to$^{w}$-l$^{e}$d-ot ’adam*
*b$^{e}$-yo$^{w}$m b$^{e}$ro’ ’$^{\varepsilon}$loh-iym ’adam . . .*

This is the book of the *to$^{w}$-l$^{e}$d-ot* of Adam
On the day of the gods’ creation of Adam . . .—

what does this show of the purpose of Genesis 2?

A *to$^{w}$-l$^{e}$d-o$^{w}$t* "genealogy" states sequence of births, for *to$^{w}$-l$^{e}$d-o$^{w}$t** is an abstract noun formed by fixing the abstract noun-forming prefix *t-* to the causative form *ho$^{w}$-liyd* of the verb *yalad* "to give birth": Arabic *walada*:

*The absolute form *to$^{w}$-l$^{e}$d-o$^{w}$t* "genealogy" is shortened to *to$^{w}$-l$^{e}$d-ot* when a qualifying word follows: *to$^{w}$-l$^{e}$d-ot ’adam* "genealogy of Adam."

*yalad* "to give birth" (as women do) *wat-te-lɛd*
*ho$^{w}$-liyd* "to cause to give birth" (as men do) *way-yo$^{w}$-led*
*to$^{w}$-l$^{e}$d-o$^{w}$t* "lists of who caused whom to be born"—a genealogical list, genealogies.

A *to$^{w}$-l$^{e}$d-o$^{w}$t* starts by taking the person whose *to$^{w}$-l$^{e}$d-o$^{w}$t* is being stated as a male parent:

*'ellɛh to$^{w}$-l$^{e}$d-ot šem*
*šem bɛn m$^{e}$'ah šanah*
*way-yo$^{w}$-lɛd 'ɛt 'ar$^{e}$pakšad*
*šenat-ayim 'aḥar ham-mab-bu$^{w}$l.*

These are the *to$^{w}$-l$^{e}$d-ot* of Shem:
When Shem was a hundred years old,
he caused Arpakshad to be born two years after the downpour [Gen. 11:10].

*w$^{e}$-'ellɛh to$^{w}$-l$^{e}$d-o$^{w}$t pɛrɛṣ*
*pɛrɛṣ ho$^{w}$-liyd 'ɛt hɛṣ$^{e}$r-o$^{w}$n. . . .*

And these are the *to$^{w}$-l$^{e}$d-ot* of *Pɛrɛṣ.*
*Pɛrɛṣ* caused *Heṣron* to be born . . . [Ruth 4:18–22].

## Creation as Giving Birth

In a *to$^{w}$-l$^{e}$d-ot* of the heavens and the earth, then, we should expect to read of the children (descendants) borne by the heavens and the earth. In traditional mythology, heaven would be the father (e.g., Igbo *Igwe*) and earth the mother (e.g., Igbo *Ala;* Fante *Asase Yaa;* Mende *Maa Ndo*) of *ha-'adam:* rain from heaven would be the semen and the inside of the earth would be the womb. The Hebrews did not like the sexual implications of this *Ba'al-ism,* and the Hebrew writers of Genesis 2 have not pursued the myth of the *to$^{w}$-l$^{e}$d-ot* of the heavens and the earth to its traditional conclusions.

In this *to$^{w}$-l$^{e}$d-ot* of the heavens and the earth, therefore, the male role of the heavens (*-iym* in Hebrew *haš-šamay-im* is a masculine plural suffix; however, when the noun itself ends in *y*, the suffix becomes *im*) has been displaced by the introduction of the agency of YHWH *('$^{ɛ}$loh-iym)* as the great spirit. We can merely glimpse the ancient mythology lurking under the theology. To introduce YHWH *'$^{\varepsilon}$loh-iym* into an ancient mythology in which the male heavens and the female earth were procreative agents—persons or spirits or gods—is to turn mythology into theology.

For a glimpse of the myths, see statements like that in Genesis 6 that *b$^{e}$n-ey ha-'$^{\varepsilon}$loh-iym* "the sons of the gods" married *b$^{e}$n-o$^{w}$t ha-'adam* "the daughters of men" and gave birth to *gibbor-iym* "powerful ones":

> *b$^{e}$n-ey ha-'$^{\varepsilon}$loh-iym + b$^{e}$n-o$^{w}$t ha-'adam → gibbor-iym*
> *haš-šamay-im + ha-'adam-ah → 'adam*

The Yahwistic writer (J) of Genesis 2 announced a myth of how the Sky God and Mother Earth gave birth through sexual copulation or insemination, but then suppressed that line of thought because myths of creation by giving birth require two divine parents, a progenitor and a progenitrix, and that is polytheism. Rather than introduce polytheism, the Yahwist switched to another imagery.

## The Creator as Plastic Artist (Genesis 2)

The firstborn of the heavens and the earth, according to Genesis 2, is *ha-'adam,* formed (*yṣr* "molded") by YHWH of *'apar* (Akkadian *eperu* "dust"; Acholi *apulu* "dust"; Yoruba *ẹ̀rọ̀fọ̀* "mud" and *erùkpẹ̀* "dust") from *ha-'adam-ah* "(top)soil" (red earth) before any *ṣiyah has-sadɛh* "wild growth" was in the earth, before any *'esɛb has-sadɛh* "herbs of the field" sprouted up (Gen. 2:5).

In the absence of plants and vegetation God provided *ha-'adam* with sustenance by planting a *gan* "fenced garden" in *'edɛn.* In this *gan* God placed *ha-'adam* and made every type of desirable and tasty fruit tree to grow. There was the *'eṣ ha-ḥayy-iym* in the middle; there was the *'eṣ had-da'at ṭo$^{w}$b wa-ra'.*

> God stationed *ha-'adam* in *gan-'edɛn*
> to till it and to watch it [Gen. 2:15].

The gardener could eat any fruit in the *gan* except from *'eṣ had-da'at ṭo$^{w}$b wa-ra'.*

To provide company for *ha-'adam* God formed (*yṣr* "molded") all the animals—also from *ha-'adam-ah,* as a *yo$^{w}$ṣer* "a potter" molds pots out of clay. They were formed by God, but they were named—assigned their callings and roles in life—by *ha-'adam:*

> *w$^{e}$-kol 'ašɛr yi-q$^{e}$ro' l-o$^{w}$ ha-'adam nɛfɛš ḥayyah*
> *hu$^{w}$' š$^{e}$m-o$^{w}$.*
>
> And whatever the *'adam* called the living being—
> that became its name [Gen. 2:19b].

When God eventually formed (*yṣr* "molded") *'išš-ah* "a woman" from a rib of *ha-'adam,* it was also *ha-'adam* who named her *'išš-ah*

> *kiy me-'iyš luqaḥ-ah zo't.*
>
> for it was from a man that this one was taken [Gen. 2:23b].

## Is the Creator a Parent or an Artist?

We have said that the announcement of "the *to$^{w}$-l$^{e}$d-ot* of the heavens and the earth" in Genesis 2:4 suggests that the heavens and the earth were autonomous creative powers—man and woman in sexual intercourse, as West African creation myths indicate:

| Ewe, Fọn, Egun | Nago Yoruba | Ilé Ifẹ̀ Yoruba | Igbo |
|---|---|---|---|
| *(Dada) Segbo* "great spirit" | *Ọbàtálá* "male heaven" | *Ọbàtálá* "male heaven" | *enu (Igwe)* "heaven, father" |
| *Sakpata* "earth" | *Odun* "earth" | *Odǔdúwà* "female earth" | *Ala* "mother earth" |

The Yahwist writer in Genesis 2 eliminated such copulating gods: what the myths say that god[s] (*'$^{\varepsilon}$loh-iym*) create through copulation, the Yahwist says God (YHWH) can do singlehandedly by operating as a plastic artist. This is how the Yahwist gave us the double-barreled name of god: *Yahweh '$^{\varepsilon}$loh-iym* (Yahweh in place of the god[s], Yahweh-which-the-myths-call-the-gods). The Yahwist writer in Genesis 2 has thus effected a demythologizing without announcing it. He has displaced polydaemonic mythology with monotheistic theology. The two gods of mythology who were displaced by Yahweh *(Yahweh ’$^{\varepsilon}$loh-iym)* are *(i) šamay-im* “heavens” (male) and *(ii) ’εrεṣ* “earth” (female). We know that *’εrεṣ* is female from the *-o$^{w}$t* suffix, which it takes in the plural. They were deposed by Yahweh.

When Yahweh proceeded to create plants he avoided employing any of them. As a plastic artist he could do even without *’εrεṣ* “earth.” He took *‘apar* from *ha-’adam-ah* (see Dinka *dom* “cultivated field”), not *‘apar* from *ha-’$^{a}$rεṣ*. The plural of *‘apar* is *‘ap$^{e}$r-o$^{w}$t:* the *-ah* in *’adam-ah* is the feminine suffix. The heavens and the earth, which mythology considered as joint creators, became mere creatures in the hand of Yahweh:

> These are the real *to$^{w}$-l$^{e}$d-ot* of the heavens and the earth—how they were caused to be created. On the day when YHWH—who-is-equal-to-*’$^{\varepsilon}$loh-iym*—made earth and heavens . . . [Gen. 2:4a].

## The Creator as Man of Authority (Genesis 1)

### *Demythologizing and Remythologizing*

In Genesis 1 the Priestly writers (P) performed the same demythologizing by declaring that the sun and the moon and the stars are not gods *(’$^{\varepsilon}$loh-iym)* but mere creatures of *’$^{\varepsilon}$loh-iym*. Among the ancient Egyptians the sun was not considered a mere creature: it was considered to be a god—*R‘ (Re, Ra)*—a very high god, head of the pantheon in *Ywnw* “Heliopolis” (“City of the sun”; cf. Isa. 19:18b). Egyptian *r‘* “sun” is Nembe Ijọ *irua* “sun,” just the light-giving star, not a god among the Ijọ as he seems to be among the Igbo, who call him *Anyanwu (anya anwu* “eyes of *anwu*”; Arabic *‘ayn šams)*.

When you demythologize the myth of any people, you kill their gods and they brand you a heretic and may even kill you. If you said among ancient Egyptians, who worshiped *Re, Ra,* and who gave their kings such titles as *Ra-mesw* “child of *Ra*” (*Ra-m$^{e}$ses*) that *re‘* “sun” is not a god, you have said to them, “Your god

(*Re*ʿ) is dead.'' They would call you an atheist, ''someone who does not believe in (our) god.'' Thus the Romans branded the early Christians atheists because the early Christians refused to believe that Caesar was a god. Mythologizers always call demythologizers atheists.

The Yahwist writers of Genesis 2 and the Priestly writers of Genesis 1 were demythologizers of ancient myths. To demythologize, you effect a drastic change in imagery. If *mythology says* that the creator is a male-female couple (e.g., *Mawu-Lisa* of the Fọn) producing by sexual intercourse, *the Yahwist says:* ''No. The creator is a single plastic artist using fine dust of the soil as plaster or clay to mold man, woman, and beasts (Gen. 2:4ff.), and *the Priestly writer says:* ''No. The creator is a spirit who merely blows the spirit from his lips as words of life and power: and sun, moon, stars, sea, land, and fish appear. The creator creates by words of power—words of command'' (Gen. 1:1ff.).

*y$^{e}$-hiy 'o$^{w}$r wa-y$^{e}$-hiy 'o$^{w}$r.*

Let light be, and light was.

This type of command, which says *Kun!* ''Be!'' *Fa-ya-kun* ''and something comes into being—comes to pass, happens,'' is what the Urhobo call *arido* ''the creative power of the spoken word.''

The Afro-Asiatic consonantal root *rdh/rdy* in Urhobo *arido* is found in Middle Egyptian *rdi* ''speak,'' *(r)di* ''cause, permit.'' It occurs as *-r$^{e}$d(-u$^{w}$)* in the Hebrew of Genesis 1:26 and 1:28:

Sprout up and multiply
Fill the earth and trample it under foot.
*u$^{w}$-r$^{e}$d-u$^{w}$* over the fish of the sea and the birds of the air. . . .

''And *r$^{e}$d-* over the fish of the sea . . . ,'' that is, speak authoritatively to them and make them do your bidding.

*Arido* is like Hebrew *mašal,* which means *(i)* ''to speak proverbially'' and *(ii)* ''to be a ruler.'' Only people in authority, e.g., elders, are allowed to speak proverbially in a gathering. Hence *moš$^{\check{e}}$l-iym b-anu$^{w}$ p$^{e}$liš$^{\check{e}}$t-iym* in Judges 15:11 is like *u$^{w}$-r$^{e}$d-u$^{w}$ bi-d$^{e}$gat hay-yam. Mšl* occurs also in Genesis 1:18: God put the sun and the moon in the firmament *li- m$^{e}$šol bay-yo$^{w}$m u$^{w}$-bal-laylah* "to hold sway during the day and during the night [respectively]." The *rdh/rdy* root occurs in Yoruba *èrèdí/ìdí* "a cause, a reason." The reason the sun comes out every morning, according to this way of thinking, is because it is obeying an *arido*—the *arido* of God. This is where the Woodaabe Fulani got their title for the lineage head: *ardo* (» *arta* "to lead").

God, says the Priestly writer of Genesis 1, is not an image-maker (Igbo *onye mgbe*). God brings things to pass by speaking authoritatively:

| | "To say" | "To command" | "To teach" | "Ruler" |
|---|---|---|---|---|
| Hebrew | *'amar* | | | |
| Arabic | | *'amar* | | *'amiyr* (» emir, admiral) |
| Hebrew | *mašal* | | | *mošɛl* (»marshal) |
| Hebrew | *hig-giyd* | | | *nagiyd* |
| Egyptian | *rdi* | | | *ardo* (Fulfulde) |
| Igbo | | | *-kuzi* | *n-kosi* (Zulu) |
| Hebrew | | | *'illef* | *'allu$^{w}$f* |

Hebrew *'amar* occurs eight times in Genesis 1. We could say that whereas in Genesis 2 (J—Yahwist writer) God is a plastic artist, in Genesis 1 (P—Priestly writers) God is an *'amiyr* "a commander" (an emir). One reason why the Priestly writer (ca. 450 B.C.) found it necessary to change the metaphor of the Yahwist (ca. 950 B.C.) is that those who believe that God is an image-maker may be inclined themselves to make images. This activity had been banned in Israel. God was therefore presented as a commander: the spirit (voice) proceeding from his lips brings things to life: "Man shall live by all that proceeds out of the mouth of God" (cf. Deut. 8:3).

We must note, however, that the remythologizing of the Priestly writer in Genesis 1 is incomplete. For the word *bara'* "he created," which occurs as the very first verb, actually suggests "to mold." At the very end of his account—Genesis 2:3b—*bara'* means "he began" (: Yoruba *bẹ̀rẹ̀* "begin"): *bara' la-'as-o$^{w}$t* "began to make." But in Genesis 1:27, *way-yi-b$^{e}$ro'* "and he created," we have a glimpse of the method of creation in *b$^{e}$-ṣal$^{e}$m-o$^{w}$* "in his image."[1] This suggests a physical model for a physical image. *'Al-baari'* "the fashioner," one of the Qur'anic titles of God, appears among the

Akan as *borebore,* one of the titles of *Onyame* "God." *Borebore* is a reduplication of Hebrew *bo$^{w}$re'* "creator" from the Afro-Asiatic root *b-r-'*. The manner of creation is shown in the Igbo reflex—*Mbari* is mud sculpture.[2]

The Priestly editors of Genesis have put the later account of creation by potent speech right at the beginning in order to let that sound the signature tune: God is a spirit; the voice from his lips is spirit. The spirit is creative. It is life.

*Naming*

Where Genesis 1 says that *'$^{ε}$loh-iym* gave human beings the commission to exercise command over the fish, the birds, and the animals, Genesis 2 says the same thing differently. It says that God brought all that he had created to *'adam* to name them. To give a thing a name is to exercise authority over the thing; to give a person a name is to acknowledge ownership of the person. Only the owner of a dog gives a dog a name. Only a conqueror of a country can change the name of the country.

What Genesis 2 means by saying that God created and then invited man to name is that man is God's assistant in the work of creation. God creates: man uses God's creation. To name something is to decide what it will be used for. The same type of vehicle from the same factory can be named "hearse" by one city council and "Black Maria" by another city council. God creates and human beings decide the use to which to put God's creation. The human being is not the creator, but the user of what God has created.

Just as Joseph was crucial in the *to$^{w}$-l$^{e}$d-ot* of *Ya'$^{a}$qob,*

> *'ellεh to$^{w}$-l$^{e}$d-ot ya'$^{a}$qob—*
> *Yo$^{w}$s$^{ε}$f bεn š$^{e}$ba'-'$^{ε}$s$^{e}$reh šanah*
> *hayah ro'εh 'εt 'εḥ-ay-w baṣ-ṣo'n,*

> These are the *to$^{w}$-l$^{e}$d-ot* of Jacob—
> Joseph, being seventeen years old,
> was shepherding with his brothers among the sheep
> [Gen. 37:1b],

so is man crucial in the *to$^{w}$-l$^{e}$d-ot* of heaven and earth. Once God had made the heavens and the earth, the next thing he did was to use *'apar* from *ha-'adam-ah* (both feminine elements of earth) to mold man—the principal actor in the *to$^w$-l$^e$d-ot* of earth, if not of the heavens. For him God made the plants to sprout. For him God molded the animals.

But as man did not make these things himself, God laid down the limits to man's use of the ecological resources of the earth. As long as man observed ecological bounds all went well—the earth brought forth its increase. When man transgressed the bounds, he lost well-watered Eden and found himself condemned to sweat on infertile soil. This is the story of desertification—how deserts were formed. This is what the story of the expulsion of *ha-'adam* and *Ḥawwah* from the *gan* in *'edɛn* was trying to account for.

When I was small I used to be surprised to read the notices on forest reserves and game reserves prohibiting cutting of trees or killing of game. "Why on earth," I used to wonder, "would the government prevent people from hunting in certain forests?" Why, we may ask concerning the prohibition about the tree of knowledge, would God protect that particular tree from human depredation?

That tree is, of course, a symbol. Human life depends on plant life. Exhaust plant life and people die. The Sahara became a desert because people cut the trees that they should have left untouched in a sort of forest reserve. The point is that people must not exploit all the resources of their environment without any reserve religiously preserved. To use all resources without reserve is to misuse ecological resources. We know now that it brings an ecological curse on people.

Who despoils the environment more, nomadic herdsmen or primitive farmers with their shifting cultivation and bush burning? Or the miners of gold, silver, iron, copper, coal, and petroleum? Which of these corresponds to *Qayin* (Cain)? Which to *Hɛbɛl* (Abel)? Which to *Tu$^w$bal-Qayin* (Tubal Cain)?

The first violence of human beings was ecological violence—unrestrained onslaught on the flora—which turned a *gan* (Hausa *gona* "farm"; Yoruba *ẹ-gàn* "virgin forest, black loamy soil") into a soil that makes the farmer sweat:

> Accursed is the ground because of you,
> In toil will you eat of it all the days of your life,
> Thorns and thistles will it bring forth for you
> And you shall eat wild plants.

With the sweat of your nose you will eat food
Until you return to the earth
From which you were taken.
You are, in any case, dust,
And to dust you will return [Gen. 3:17b–19].

# 2

# The *to$^{w}$-l$^{e}$d-ot* of Adam

*zɛh sefɛr to$^{w}$-l$^{e}$d-ot 'adam:*
*b$^{e}$-yo$^{w}$m b$^{e}$ro' '$^{ɛ}$loh-iym ha-'adam*
*bi-d$^{e}$m-u$^{w}$t '$^{ɛ}$loh-iym 'asah 'ot-o$^{w}$.*

This is the book of the *to$^{w}$-l$^{e}$d-ot* of Adam:
On the day when the gods created the Adam,
It was in the *d$^{e}$m-u$^{w}$t* of gods that he made him
[Gen. 5:1–2].

The genealogical tree (*to$^{w}$-l$^{e}$d-ot*) then goes on: *'Adam* → *Šet* → *'$^{ɛ}$no$^{w}$š* → *Qeynan* → *Ma-halal 'el* → *Yɛrɛd* → *Ḥano$^{w}$k* → *M$^{e}$tu$^{w}$šɛ-laḥ* → *Lamɛk* → *Noaḥ*. After Noah, his three sons were listed: *Šem, Ḥam,* and *Yafɛt*. Then came the flood, bringing to an end the history before the flood.

### *'$^{ɛ}$no$^{w}$š—ben 'adam*

Which Hebrew word means "human being"—Adam or Enosh? Hebrew uses the word *'$^{ɛ}$no$^{w}$š* in poetic passages in synonymous parallelism to the phrase *bɛn 'adam* "son of *'adam*":

*mah '$^{ɛ}$no$^{w}$š . . .*
*u$^{w}$ bɛn 'adam . . . ?*

What is *'$^{ɛ}$no$^{w}$š . . .*
Or *bɛn 'adam* . . . [Ps. 8:4]?

Enosh, then, is *bɛn ’adam*: Enosh is “man,” “human being”; *’adam* is not. Hebrew ’$^{\varepsilon}$*no*$^{w}$*š*, like Aramaic *’enaš* and Arabic *’in*$^{e}$*s-aan*, means “human being.”[1]

’$^{\varepsilon}$*no*$^{w}$*š* is not *’adam*. In Hebrew poetry *’adam* occurs in parallelism with *gɛbɛr*[2] (Job 14:10), while *bɛn ’adam* occurs in parallelism with ’$^{\varepsilon}$*no*$^{w}$*š* (Ps. 8:5). Whereas ’$^{\varepsilon}$*no*$^{w}$*š* has plural forms (masculine *’anaš-iym* and feminine *naš-iym*), *’adam* is unique. It has no plural form. And its feminine form does not mean “woman”: Hebrew *’adam-ah* is “soil.” *’Adam* has no human father and no human mother. Can we really call such a being an ordinary human being? He is not *y*$^{e}$*lu*$^{w}$*d ’iššah* “one born of woman” (Job 25:4). When *’adam* is used in Job to mean “man,” specification is given: *’adam y*$^{e}$*lu*$^{w}$*d ’iššah* “*’adam* born of woman” (Job 14:1a), implying that there are other *’adam* not born of woman. *’Adam* in Job is not even “first human being,” for that one needed also to be specified: *ri’š-o*$^{w}$*n ’adam*, “ancestral” *’adam* (:Yoruba *Àdàmú òrìṣà*).

The basic meaning of the Afro-Asiatic root *’-d-m* is that quality which is manifested in reddish-brown, tawny creatures like the lion (Igbo *odum*[3]), the bear (nicknamed *Bruno*[4]), the python (Ijọ *odum*; Fọn *dã*), the tree *Chlorophora excelsa* (Twi *odum*). What the ancients found to be common to all of these was vitality—life force. This same life principle was discerned in blood (Hebrew *dam*) and in red soil (Hebrew *’adam-ah*).[5] It is this abstraction that the Hebrew abstract noun *d*$^{e}$*m-u*$^{w}$*t* is meant to capture.[6] If ’$^{\varepsilon}$*loh-iym* said, “Let us make *’adam* like our own *d*$^{e}$*m-u*$^{w}$*t*” (Gen. 1:26), it is this life principle, this vitality, that is being thought of as the pattern, not a *ta-b*$^{e}$*n-iyt* “an image” (Ps. 106:20b). The strongest of animals and trees share this superhuman *d*$^{e}$*m-u*$^{w}$*t*. They differ in *ta-b*$^{e}$*n-iyt*.[7] The ancients rubbed red ochre on the dead as a way to wish them renewed vitality; and priests tried to present themselves before deities in the *d*$^{e}$*m-u*$^{w}$*t* of gods by rubbing themselves with red ochre. In sacrifice a cow may be slaughtered, but the meat—the flesh—is not offered to the gods. What is offered to the gods is the red stuff and the white stuff—the life blood and the fat.

Genesis 9:4–6 is the *locus classicus* for determining what *d*$^{e}$*m-u*$^{w}$*t* meant to the ancient Hebrews. People may eat the flesh of animals but not their *nɛfɛš*, their *dam*:

He who sheds the *dam* of *’adam*, by *’adam* will his *dam* be shed
For it is in the *ṣɛlɛm* of *’$^ε$loh-iym* that he made the *’adam*
[Gen. 9:6].

There is a morphological signal in the homophonic assonance of this gnomic statement: as *dam* is to *’adam*, so is *d$^e$m-u$^w$t* to *’$^ε$loh-iym*. Progenitors pass both to their offspring—the tangible *dam* and the intangible *d$^e$m-u$^w$t*:

When Adam was one hundred and thirty years old,
he caused a son to be born in his *d$^e$m-u$^w$t*, like his *ṣɛlɛm*
[Gen. 5:3].

The double entendre in Genesis 9:6 is gnomic; for it is possible that a man may shed the *dam* of *bɛn ’adam* and his own *dam* may not be shed by *’adam y$^e$lu$^w$d ’iššah*. But it is the belief of the ancients that one day his own *dam* will be shed by *’adam* (a lion or a python or a monkey or a bat or an *odum* tree). It was presumably of the *odum* tree that the Yoruba spoke when they said:

*Ọmọdé bú ìrókò, ó b’ ojú w’ ẹ̀hìn:*
*O ṣebí ọjọ́ kan náà l’ ó ń pa ènìyàn?*

A youth abused the *odum* and looked over his shoulder:
You think it is on the same day that it kills *’$^ε$no$^w$š*?

When *Qayin* shed the *dam* of *Hɛbɛl* there was no other *’adam* there to see him. But *’adam-ah*, the mother of all *b$^e$n-o$^w$t ’adam*, was there and got soaked in the *dam*. It was through her that Yahweh *’$^ε$loh-iym* became aware of what *Qayin* had done:

The call of the *dam-iym* of your *ẹ̀hì* is shouting to me from *’adam-ah*.
Now, accursed are you from the *’adam-ah*
which opened her mouth with an oath
to receive the *dam-iym* of your *ẹ̀hì* from your hand.
If you till the *’adam-ah* laboriously,
she will no longer give you its vitality . . .
[Gen. 4:10–12].[8]

It is not surprising that to parallel *’adam* in Hebrew poetry the word used is *gεbεr*, from the same root as Hebrew *gᵉbuʷr-ah* and Yoruba *a-gbára* “power.” In Hebrew *gabᵉr-iy ’el*, the *gebre* of God, is not a human being but an angel.[9] The reflex in Yoruba mythology is twofold: *(i) Ẹl-ẹ́-gbara*, the messenger of *Ọrunmila* “heaven knows salvation” (the oracle divinity, Igbo *A-gbara/ A-gbala;* Fọn *Lεgba*) and *(ii) e-gbére,* a diminutive but powerful manlike creature of the forest—a daemon. If an *ènìyàn (’εnoʷš)* encounters an *e-gbére (gεbεr)* in the forest, the *ènìyàn* is sure to lose. For *gεbεr (’adam)* is older (i.e., stronger) than *’ᵉnoʷš (bεn ’adam)*.

The Yoruba say of *egbére*:

*Kò ṣ’ eran-ko;*
*Kò ṣ’ ènìyàn.*

He is not a beast;
He is not a human being.

Twi *odum* refers to the tree *Chlorophora excelsa,* which is not only the tallest of African trees but the one whose wood is hardest. It is red wood. *Odum*, the Twi name for this tree, points to its strength and the reddish color of its wood; *ìrókò, logo, loko*—as it is known by the Yoruba, the Ewe-Aja-Gεn-Fọn, and the Igbo—point to its height/length. For *ìrókò* is from the same root as Hebrew *’arak* “be long,” *’orεk* “length.” “This huge tree is venerated as the seat of the invisible powers of the Forest.”[10]

The Igbo believe that the invisible spirits inhabiting the *ìrókò* sometimes get inside a pregnant woman to be born as *ogbanje* (Yoruba *emèrè, eléèré*), children with playmates in the spirit world with whom they had made a compact to return after a short stay in the world of human beings. These are the *àbíkú* of Yoruba superstition—children born to die. These sons of *ìrókò* can be truly regarded as *bᵉn-ey ha-’adam*. They are, of course, petted, as one appeases the *òrìṣà* “divine ancestor.”

If *gεbεr* is an *e-gbére, ’adam* is an *ẹ-bọra*. Yoruba *ẹ-bọra* is *(i)* a spirit, and *(ii)* a terra-cotta image *(ẹbọra rere mà l’ ère)*. For *(i)* Arabic has *’al-bariy’*, Hebrew *boʷre’,* Twi *Borebore*—all of them titles of God as creator (Hebrew *bara’* “create”; Efik *boro* "mold"). For *(ii)* Arabic has *bir$^{e}$'ah* "creature," Igbo *Mbari* "artwork." Such an artistic creation is *'adam*, as we read in Genesis 2. He is an *ẹbọra,* not an *ènìyàn.*

To become an *ẹbọra,* a man has to die and become an ancestor living in spirit (asexual) but no longer in body (sexually differentiated). Then a terra-cotta head is made in his image. Hence the terra-cotta heads of Ilé Ifẹ̀. The soapstone images at Esie are worshiped as *ẹbọra* and propitiation is made to them by persons wanting to have children.[11] For *'adam* is the principle behind all life—the self-reproducing force.

## *Àdàmú Òrìṣà*

There is a funereal ceremony of the *Àhólì/Àwórì* in Lagos called *Ẹ̀yọ̀* or *Àdàmú Òrìṣà.* A few years after the death of a famous man or woman, the relatives ask the *ọba* for permission to perform the *Ẹ̀yọ̀ (Àdàmú Òrìṣà)* ceremony so that the *Ẹ̀yọ̀* may come out and take to themselves the soul of the departed. Thus, it is believed, the departed will join the ancestors in the world of the undying spirits. The *Ẹ̀yọ̀* are masquerades and, as in other West African societies, they represent long-dead ancestors who come back to visit their descendants (see Yoruba *egúngún*; Efik *ekpe*; Ebira *Eku*; Idoma *Ekwu*; "masks, masquerades"). In the *Ẹ̀yọ̀* ceremony, up to two thousand *Ẹ̀yọ̀* masquerades may fill the streets of Lagos.

The first *Ẹ̀yọ̀* to come out in the morning is the eldest—the most senior—called *Àdàmú Òrìṣà.* The name gives away the fact that this is *ri'š-o$^{w}$n 'adam*—Adam No. 1; for Yoruba *òrìṣà* "patron saints, divine ancestors" *(-r-ṣ-)* is from the same *r'š* root as Hebrew *ha-ri'š-o$^{w}$n* "the first." *Ha-ri'š-on-iym* in Psalm 79:8 is rendered "the ancestors" in the Jerusalem Bible. There are two reflexes of the Afro-Asiatic root *r'š* in Yoruba *(i) Rísà, Lísà, Olísà* "chief of first rank" (Hebrew *ro'š* "chief"; Arabic *ra'iys* "president"; Amharic *ras* "Duke"; Acholi *rwot, ruoth* "chief") and *(ii) òrìṣà* "patron saints, divine ancestors, divinities" (Hebrew *ri'š-on-iym*);[12] *(i)* is a historical category—chiefs; *(ii)* is a concept in mythology—gods.

The following *ri'š-on-iym (òrìṣà)* are mentioned in Genesis 5: *'adam (Àdàmú Òrìṣà), Šet, '$^{\varepsilon}$no$^{w}$š (ènìyàn), Qeynan, Ma-halal'el,*

*Yɛrɛd, Ḥano$^w$k (Nok), M$^e$tu$^w$-šɛlaḥ* "spearman" (Hebrew *m$^e$t-u$^w$* "man of" = Bantu *ntu* "life"; Igbo *ndu* "life," *madu;* Hausa *mut-um* "man, person"; Hebrew *šɛlaḥ* "dart" = Zulu *i-sikhal* "weapon"; Swahili *m-šale* "arrow"), *Lamɛk, Noaḥ*. From Genesis 4 we should add the line of *Qayin,* which has been "banned" from the list in Genesis 5:

*Qayin,* the first farmer, first builder of a village/town/city (Yoruba *Ògún*), father of *Ḥano$^w$k (Nok)*
*'Iyrad, M$^e$-hu$^w$ya'el, M$^e$tu$^w$ša'el* and *Lamɛk*
*Tu$^w$bal Qayin,* the first peripatetic smith (Hahm *Kuno;* Ebira *Egene*)
*Yabal,* the first nomadic tent-dweller and his *nwa nne*
*Yu$^w$bal,* the first itinerant musician (Hebrew *yo$^w$bɛl* "horn of a ram"; Igbo *ebulu* "ram"; Acholi *bila*; Gã *bla*; Twi *abɛn* "horn").
*Hɛbɛl,* the first shepherd *(Fula, Pulo)* died childless, eliminated by *Qayin* in the struggle for the survival of the fittest. He was reincarnated later as *'Ebɛr, Abore, Bororo.*

All these would be recorded by the Yoruba as *òrìṣà*, and the myths about them would give the impression that sometimes they were *òrìṣà* "divine spirits"—thunder, lightning, fire, iron—and sometimes that they were *Rísà, Lísà, Olísà*—human chiefs. Thus is Adam both a totemic and a divine ancestor. And thus is *Qayin* both an *'iyš* and a *Yɛhwe*. When the Yoruba call the Egba Yoruba *ọmọ Líṣàbi* "children of *Líṣàbi*," it should be noted that *Líṣà-bi* himself is a descendant of *Líṣà*.

We can group all the characters in the Bible before Abram as mythological. All the "living things" that were destroyed in the flood were called "all the *y$^e$qu$^w$m* that were on the face of the *'adam-ah*—from *'adam* to beasts to reptiles to birds of the sky" (Gen. 7:23). Hebrew *y$^e$qu$^w$m* is cognate with Ngas *qum* "spirit" and Yoruba *egúngún* "ancestral masks" (representing dead ancestors come back to life). With Abram, legend begins. History perhaps does not begin until David appointed a recorder *(sofɛr)* among his palace officials. The first historians among any people usually consider it their task to begin from the beginning. They thus fill prehistoric gaps with poetic myths and legendary sagas.

Adam, then, is *ri'š$^{\gamma}$-o$^{w}$n 'adam* (*Àdàmú òrìṣà,* Job 15:7), generated directly from *'adam-ah* by *YHWH '$^{\varepsilon}$loh-iym*. It is this *òrìṣà* who comes back as the most senior of the *Ẹ̀yọ̀* (: Hebrew *ḥay*[13]) at an *Àdàmú Òrìṣà* celebration to take away a recently dead *gibbo$^{w}$r* to be gathered unto his people.

## *Ḥano$^{w}$k*—Nok

And *Ḥano$^{w}$k* walked with the gods
  and he became nonexistent,
For the gods took him [away] [Gen. 5:24].

This *Ḥano$^{w}$k* is not the descendant of Adam through accursed *Qayin*, the one after whom *Qayin* named the city that he built (Gen. 4:17). The *Ḥano$^{w}$k* who walked with the gods was the descendant of Adam through Seth and Enosh (Gen. 5). This *Ḥano$^{w}$k*

walked with the gods
  and he was not.

Margaret Field has an interesting explanation for how *Ḥano$^{w}$k* was spirited away.[14] *W$^{e}$-'eyn-ɛn-nu$^{w}$* "and he was not" is a euphemism for "and he died" (Yoruba *ó ṣe al-âì-sí* "he became an is-not"). *Ḥano$^{w}$k*, like all those whom the gods love, died young (365 years compared with his son's 969 years). It is clear that neither *Ḥano$^{w}$k* nor *M$^{e}$t-u$^{w}$š$^{\gamma}$ɛlaḥ* was a human being; they should be taken as groups of peoples, not as individual persons.

Hebrew *Ḥano$^{w}$k* is transcribed in the English versions as Enoch. The phonological correspondence with Chadic languages points to the placename *Nok* as the West African reflex of the biblical *Ḥano$^{w}$k*, the descendant of Adam through *Qayin* (*Ògún*, the Yoruba patron saint of agriculture and iron working). To say that *Qayin* called the name of the city he built after the name of *Ḥano$^{w}$k*, his son, is to say that the discovery of the use of iron by *Ògún* made Nok civilization possible. Nok civilization in the Jos plateau of Nigeria is considered by archeologists to be the earliest civilization in the central Sudan.[15]

The Hahm people of northern Nigeria are in the area of Nok. Byang Kato, himself a Hahm, tells us that in the Hahm language

*Nok* probably means "to start"[16] (cf. Igbo *neke* "creator"; Hebrew *nkḥ* "be in front"; Yoruba *kọ́* "be first").

> The spirits are always associated with "Kuno," Satan. Jaba have never doubted the existence or activities of Satan. He is a real person to them. Iron smelting is an old trade in Jaba land. Evidences of hearths built generations ago can be seen all over the area. Legends are told of the hearths being old mansions of Satan. Before the advent of missions, it was a taboo to dig up any of the furnace hearths. People firmly believed that if a person dug out the hearth, he would become mad.[17]

Jaba is the name the Hausa call the Hahm of Nok who consider *Kuno* to be the inventor of iron smelting. They consider *Kuno* to be an evil genius—Satan; but this is simply the misconception of the common people or of an age that no longer practices the ancient science of iron smelting and therefore no longer understands the origin of the furnace hearths.[18] *Ḥawwah* called her first son *Qayin*, for she thought she had got not only an *'iyš* "man" but also a *YHWH* "spirit." Hahm *Kuno* is simply *Qayin*: he was a city builder, a founder of a civilization. He named his city Nok.

# 3

# The Sons of the Gods and the Daughters of Men

Who are the *b$^{e}$n-ey ha-'$^{\varepsilon}$loh-iym* "sons of the gods" who, seeing that *b$^{e}$n-ot ha-'adam* "the daughters of men" were *ṭob-ot* "good" (i.e., beautiful), chose wives from among them (Gen. 6:1–2)? *B$^{e}$n-ey ha-'$^{\varepsilon}$loh-iym* are "divine men" (men of noble birth); *b$^{e}$n-ot ha-'adam* are human women. It is here postulated that the *gibbor-iym* (Yoruba *al-ágbára* "powerful men"), that is, "heroes" whose achievements suggested superhuman power, must have had a superhuman ancestry: one of their parents or both must be divine.

Which one could it be? In mythologies of creation through birth, the male partner comes from the sky (rain from the sky = semen), while the female partner comes from the earth (Mother Earth = womb): hence sons of the gods (in heaven) and daughters of men (on earth). It will be hard to find the opposite in mythology anywhere: sons of men marrying daughters of gods. Egyptian cosmogony is one exception: *Geb* "the earth" is made masculine, while *Nut* "the sky" is made feminine.

This way of thinking led to the attribution of the paternity of Jesus to heaven (God, the Holy Spirit) while his mother was of this earth *(Mir$^{e}$yam)*. One is not expected to be able to point to a man (a human being) as the father of a hero (see Otto Rank, *The Myth of the Birth of the Hero)*. Those who resented the title *bεn ha-'$^{\varepsilon}$loh-iym* "son of God" for Jesus did so partly because they could say: "Is this not the son of Joseph?"

## *Hag-gibbor-iym*

Who were the *gibbor-iym* "powerful men"? They were *'on$^{e}$š-ey haš-šem* "the men of fame," the famous men who lived of old (Gen. 6:4). For example, there is Shaka, king of the Zulu. How did he get such strength, such power, such charisma? Who was his father? How are such men born? The theory (the myth) of the sons of the gods and the daughters of men was offered as an explanation for the supernatural—the extraordinary—military performance of famous warriors of old. They are, therefore, referred to as *n$^{e}$fil-iym* "fallen people" (« *nafal* "fall")—those who descended upon earth from heaven.

The first of such persons spoken of in the Bible is *Nim$^{e}$rod,* known in Yoruba legend as *Lámúrúdù:*

> He was the first to be a *gibbor* on earth.
> He was a mighty hunter in the presence of Yahweh.
> For which reason it used to be said: "Like Nimrod
> a mighty hunter in the presence of Yahweh" [Gen. 10:8–9].

### Gibbor-iym *as Threats to the Gods*

Because *gibbor-iym* have in them the double potentialities of their divine/human ancestry, they frequently attempt superhuman projects, which encroach on the domain of the gods. The gods, therefore, become jealous of the exploits of the *gibbor-iym.* It is this that explains Genesis 6:5: "And God saw that the evil of *'adam* was spreading on earth and that all the artistic dreams and mental thoughts of his heart were simply evil every day."

Nothing else was alleged against man. The only evil we can see is physical (military) ambition to achieve on a superhuman level. Note that this attempt to transcend limits set for creatures was the primal evil that *'adam* and *Ḥawwah* were accused of. It was not sex, for without that they could not be fruitful and multiply. It was snatching at classified knowledge through unbridled research. It was the fault that marked Dr. Faustus: intellectual ambition. It is the crime of witchcraft: a tree that produces both good witchcraft and bad witchcraft, each of them special knowledge. It is the "sin" of divination, which depends on riddle and equivocation. Hebrew *nahaš* is "serpent," but Hebrew *niḥeš* is "to practice divination."

The serpent in Eden hinted at this jealousy by the gods of the divine aspirations of heroic men when he said to *Ḥawwah:* "I assure you, you will not die. The truth is that *'ᵉloh-iym* are aware that on the day you eat of it your eyes will be opened and you will be like *'ᵉloh-iym*—knowing good and evil" (Gen. 3:4b–5).

The gods do not want human beings to know everything—good and evil—as witches and wizards are reputed to do and as diviners aspire to do. The witch who can stop rain or make rain is already trying to be a god—omniscient and omnipotent. The gods do not like it. In Greek mythology, when Icarus flew too near the sun, the sun melted the wax of his wings and he fell into the sea. It is for this that the gods decided to put *ha-'adam* and *Ḥawwah* in their place by excluding them from access to the ultimate divine attribute—immortality.

The only difference between human beings and gods is that human beings die but gods do not: human beings are mortal; gods are immortal. As for intellectual ability, human beings have eaten of the fruit of the tree of the knowledge of good and evil and have been described by the gods themselves: "Evidently, the *'adam* has become like one of us [in the ability] to know good and evil" (Gen. 3:22). The brilliant scientific achievement of human beings is evidence of human intellectual ability; the failure of the attempts to find the elixir of life is evidence of human mortality.

## Nimᵉrod, *the First Emperor*

From Genesis 10:9b,

> For which reason there is the saying,
> "Like Nimrod a *gibbor ṣayid* [mighty hunter] before Yahweh,"

we see what was meant by calling the *gibbor-iym* men of fame, that is, *'onᵉš-ey haš-šem* (Igbo *onye aha*). The name of Nimrod was well known in Hebrew legend. If anyone was a strong hunter, he was said to be as great a hunter as Nimrod. In antiquity the hunters were the permanently armed persons.

Nimrod was not a Semite (descendant of Shem), nor a descendant of Yafet.

> The sons of Ham (were) Kush
> and the two lands of Egypt
> and Punt
> and Canaan [Gen. 10:6].
>
> And Kush gave birth to Nimrod [Gen. 10:8a].

Nimrod, then, was a descendant of Ham. His father(land) was Kush, present-day northern Sudan. We know that the *Y^e^hu^w^d-iym* (Jews) who were relating this mythology did not bless Ham and his descendants. In fact, they attributed to them a divine curse that they would be slaves of slaves.[1]

But they were aware that these Hamites had in times past produced great men. Nimrod (Yoruba *Lámúrúdù*[2]), the first *gibbo^w^r* (Yoruba *al-ágbára* "possessor of power"), was a Kushite, and Kush was in that part of Africa now occupied by the republic of Sudan. The Dinka and the Shilluk (Nilotic Sudanese) are the tallest people in the whole world. Isaiah knew of them:

> Ah, land of whirring wings which is beyond the rivers
> of Kush,
> Which sends ambassadors by the Nile
> in vessels of papyrus upon the waters:
> Go, you swift messengers,
> to a nation, tall and smooth,
> to a people feared near and far,
> a nation mighty and conquering,
> whose land the waters divide [Isa. 18:1–2].

The description is repeated in verse 7:

> At that time gifts will be brought to the
> Lord of hosts from a people tall and smooth,

from a people feared near and far,
a nation mighty and conquering,
whose lands the waters divide. . . .

These people, tall and smooth, who live beyond the rivers of Kush are the Shilluk and the Dinka.

> To the nineteenth and even the mid-twentieth century travelers, the Dinka were better known as "giants about seven feet tall who, like the Nile Cranes, stand on one foot in the river for hours looking for fish."
>
> The land of the Dinka is in the rich Savannah, segmented by the waters of the Nile and its tributaries. Large in numbers, widespread in settlement, and divided by many rivers. . . .[3]

In Genesis 10:10–12 we read:

> The main section of the Kingdom of Nimrod was Babel [Babylon] and Erek, and Akkad [Akkadia] and Calneh in the land of *Sin*$^{e}$*'ar*. From that country emerged *'Aššu*$^{w}$*r* [Assyria], and the Assyrians built [the cities of] Nineveh and *Rehob-ot 'iyr* and Calah, and Resen between Nineveh and Calah, which is a great city.

Given this impression of the anterior greatness of the Kushite Nimrod, the first *gibbor,* the writers of Genesis did with Nimrod what they did with Nebuchadnessar: for no reason other than his greatness they stated that Nimrod's greatness was offensive to God.

The fact is that the Jews had never been great (except during the empire of David and Solomon). On the contrary, they had suffered from great nations, many of them here included in the kingdom (empire) of Nimrod: *(i)* Babylonians *(Babɛl, 'Erɛk, 'Akkad, Kal*$^{e}$*nɛh)*; *(ii)* Assyrians (Nineveh, *Rehob-ot 'iyr, Kalah, Rɛsɛn)*.

Genesis 10:8–12 virtually states that the first empire (imperialism) was that of the black man. The Jews hated this imperialism.

We must not forget that the land of Egypt, which to the Hebrews was the house of bondage, was

> *miṣ^e r-ayim b^e- 'ɛrɛṣ ḥam.*
>
> The Two Lands of *Miṣr* in the land of Ham,
> Upper and Lower Egypt in the land of Ham.

Whatever doubt there may be about the color of the original inhabitants of Lower Egypt (northern Egypt) no one doubts that Upper Egypt (southern Egypt) has always been the land of the blacks: Kush (Merowe, Nubia—present-day northern Sudan). *Mošɛh* (Moses) became used to blacks in Egypt where he was born. In fact, he married a Kushite woman, thereby incurring the criticism of his sister, Miriam, and his brother, Aaron.*

## *Kòso*

It has been suggested that *Kush* is the same word that we find in the name of the kingdom of *Ṣàngó—Ọba Kòso* "the king of *Kòso*." This suggestion offers an alternative to the folk explanation that breaks *Kòso* into two Yoruba words—*Kò so* "he did not hang"—a statement then given context in the legend of the hanging of *Ṣàngó*, the fourth Alaafin of *Ọyọ*, as legend says. The reader must choose here which is more plausible: *(i)* the historical explanation that the Yoruba were one of the Kushites who migrated westward toward the land of the sunset (Hebrew *'ɛrɛb, ma-'^e rab;* Greek *Ereb-os,* Europa; Arabic *ma-g^e rɛb;* in West Africa *Yorùbá).* This explanation pinpoints three lands toward the *ma-'^e rab* "the regions of sunset and dark night" westward from the land of Canaan (see map on p. 29): north of the Mediterranean—Europe (*Ereb-os,* Europa); south of the Mediterranean—the *Ma-g^e rɛb;* south of the Sahara—*Yorùbá.* The Kushites who migrated westward reestablished their kingdom in *Kòso* just as later the *Ọ̀yọ́* who fled from *Ọ̀yọ́ Ilé* near the Niger reestablished the kingdom north of present-day Ibadan, Nigeria (see map on p. 77).

*For further views on the Nimrod/Kush problem, see the Appendix, section I, "Nimrod."

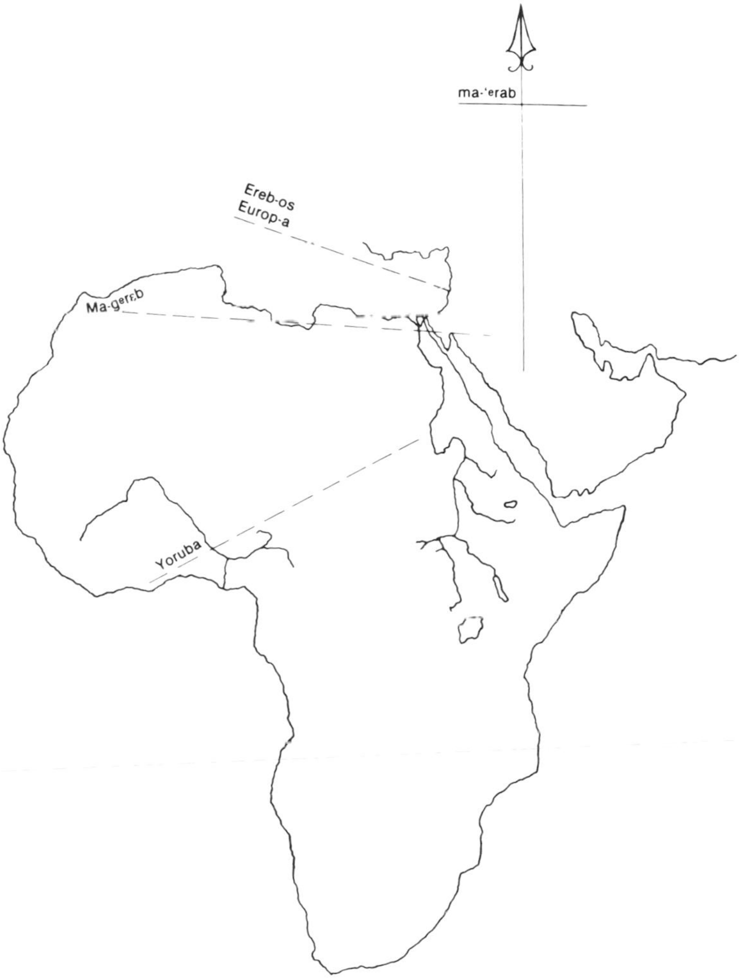


The Lands toward the Sunset

Or *(ii)* the folk explanation that the name *Kòso* derived from a decree of the supporters of *Ṣàngó,* who issued an edict that no one should spread the news that *Ṣàngó* committed suicide by hanging and issued the statement, *Ọba kò so* ''The king did not hang.''

Yoruba *Ṣàngó (š-n-g),* the *òrìṣà* of lightning and thunder, is named from an Afro-Asiatic root found in:

| | | | |
|---|---|---|---|
| Hebrew | *šɛlɛg, šal*$^{e}$*g-* | ''snow(white)'' | *(š-l-g)* |
| Aramaic | *t*$^{e}$*lag* | ''snow(white)'' | *(t-l-g)* |
| Dinka | *Deng* | ''rain, divinity of lightning'' | *(d-n-g)* |
| Acholi | *Ceng* | ''sun(shine)'' | *(č-n-g)* |
| Duala | *sang* | ''pure, holy'' | *(s-n-g)* |
| Yoruba | *Ṣàngó* | ''*òrìṣà* of lightning and thunder'' | *(š-n-g)* |
| Yoruba | *Ṡaluga* | ''spirit of cowrie shell'' | *(s-l-g)* |

The fourth *Ọba* of *Ọyọ* acquired the appelation *Ṣàngó* because of his fiery disposition, the trait that led to the rebellion of his officers, which trapped him into suicide. There was no way of being an emperor in antiquity without being a fiery warrior. The *gibbor-iym* were violent types who blazed like lightning and boomed like thunder. Because of them the earth was filled with *ḥamaṣ* ''violence'' (Gen. 6:11b, 13).

## *B*$^{e}$*n-ey ha-'*$^{\varepsilon}$*loh-iym*

> The sons and daughters of *Naa Nyọmọ* [Gã ''Father God''] are known as *jẹmawọ̃ji* ''the gods of the world.'' They are powerful and intelligent beings who walk about the world, but they have their own abodes in the sea, lagoons, mountains and other natural objects. Having been delegated by *Naa Nyọmọ* to be his vice-gerents, they are in active contact with the world of nature in men.

This quotation is from Joshua N. Kudadjie, ''Aspects of Religion and Morality in Ghanaian Traditional Society with Particular Reference to the Gã—Adangme.'' Now let us turn to Job 1:6:

> Now there was a day when *b*$^{e}$*n-*$^{e}$*y ha-'*$^{\varepsilon}$*loh-iym* [''the sons of the lords''] came to present themselves before YHWH and *Saṭan* also came among them. . . .

Who are these "sons of the lords"? The Septuagint says they are *hoi angeloi tou theou* "the messengers of God." The answer here given is that they are divine beings like *Śaṭan* (= Ngas *go sot* "the people of knowledge and power").[4] One example of *b*$^{e}$*n-ey ha-*$^{\text{'}\varepsilon}$*loh-iym,* as we have seen, is Nimrod—a great man because of physical power. The example now given in Job 1:6 is Satan—a great person because of knowledge.

We cannot escape the answer that *b*$^{e}$*n-ey ha-*$^{\text{'}\varepsilon}$*loh-iym* in Genesis 6 refers to the same divine beings whom the Gã of Ghana know as *jẹmawọ̃ji,* whom the Akan of Ghana know as *a-bọsọm (abọsọm Onyamẹ maa,* "the *a-bọsọm* are children of *Onyamẹ").*

The two examples named in Genesis and Job (Nimrod and the *Śaṭan*) are reflected in West Africa *(i)* as Yoruba *Lámúrúdù,* a legendary hero, and *(ii)* as Ngas *go sot* "persons of knowledge and power," mythological beings. In Yoruba these would be the *òrìṣà: Ènìyàn ni í d' òrìṣà* "It is human beings who become *òrìṣà.*" Hence:

| | |
|---|---|
| *Odǔdúwà* | *(i)* the first *Ọ̀ọ̀ni* of *Ilé Ifẹ̀* (legend) |
| | *(ii)* the female *òrìṣà* who, as wife of *Ọbàtálá,* gave birth to human beings at *Ilé Ifẹ̀* (myth) |
| *Ṣàngó* | *(i)* the fourth *Aláàfin* of *Ọyọ* (legend) |
| | *(ii)* the male *òrìṣà* whose anger is manifested in lightning and thunder (myth) |
| *Ọya* | *(i)* the wife of *Ṣàngó* (legend) |
| | *(ii)* the goddess of the river Niger (myth) |
| *Ògún* | *(i)* the first *ọba* of Ire in *Ekiti* (legend) |
| | *(ii)* the *òrìṣà* of iron and iron workers (myth) |

*B*$^{e}$*n-ey ha-*$^{\text{'}\varepsilon}$*loh-iym* are *hag-gibbor-iym 'ašεr me-'o*$^{w}$*lam* "the powerful men who existed from eternity" or *'an*$^{e}$*š-ey haš-šem* "the renowned human beings." There is no way of telling the story of people who existed *me-'o*$^{w}$*lam* "in the unknown distant past" except in myth. To translate Hebrew *me-'o*$^{w}$*lam* as "olden days" may give an impression of A.D. 1800 or A.D. 1500 or even 586 B.C. Hebrew *me-'o*$^{w}$*lam w*$^{e}$*-'ad 'o*$^{w}$*lam* means "from eternity to eternity." We cannot give a date to the time when the *gibbor-iym (b*$^{e}$*n-ey ha-*$^{\text{'}\varepsilon}$*loh-iym)* existed. We cannot talk about them in history books. We can learn about them only through myths.

It is in mythology that we speak of ‘‘(spiritual) lords’’ in the plural *(’$^{\varepsilon}$loh-iym)* and of sons of the ‘‘(spiritual) lords’’ *(b$^{e}$n-ey ha-’$^{\varepsilon}$loh-iym)* in the plural. Primitive religions thought in myths. Then we speak of mythology. When all these *Yεhwe* ‘‘spirits’’ are discerned as in fact one single spirit, the plurality of powers are integrated into a single God and all the powerful effectiveness of *b$^{e}$n-ey ha-’$^{\varepsilon}$loh-iym* is assigned to *bεn ha-’$^{\varepsilon}$loh-iym* ‘‘the son of God.’’ Then we speak of theology.

That the *Śaṭan* is a *gibbor* can be seen in the fact that *Ѐṣù,* the *òrìṣà* who fills the role of the *Śaṭan* in Yoruba mythology, is also known as *Ẹl-ẹ́-gbara* (Fọn *Lεgba,* cf. Ebira *nεgba* ‘‘spirit’’). Yoruba *Ẹl-ẹ́-gbara* is a byform of Yoruba *al-á-gbára* ‘‘powerful one’’ and a cognate of Amharic *gebre* ‘‘messenger, servant’’:

*al-á-gbára* (*hoi huioi tou theou*—human, legendary), e.g., *Lámúrúdù*
*Ẹl-ẹ́-gbara* (*hoi angeloi tou theou*—spirit, mythical), i.e., *Ѐṣù*
*e-gbére* (—spirit, mythical)
*a-gbára* (‘‘power’’ —Hebrew *g$^{e}$bu$^{w}$r-ah*)

*Ѐṣù Ẹlẹ́gbara* is not ‘‘the devil.’’ He is the messenger of *Ọ̀rúnmìlà,* the oracle spirit. *Lεgba* is the only one among the *vodũ* ‘‘gods’’ who can speak all the languages of all the *vodũ.* He is therefore the interpreter among them. And he interprets (intercedes) for human beings with any of the *vodũ* or even with *Mawu* ‘‘God.’’ When *b$^{e}$n-ey ha-’$^{\varepsilon}$loh-iym* presented themselves before YHWH in heaven (Job 1:6) and YHWH asked where Satan was coming from, Satan said: ‘‘From shuttling to and fro on earth and from roaming about on it.’’ *B$^{e}$n-ey ha-’$^{\varepsilon}$loh-iym,* then, could move to and fro between heaven and earth. After all, their father’s home is in heaven, and their mother’s home is among human beings. A belief in the possibility of such beings is definitely a mythical belief.

The Septuagint renders *b$^{e}$n-ey ha-’$^{\varepsilon}$loh-iym* into Greek as *hoi angeloi tou theou* ‘‘the messengers of God’’ in Job 1:6 but as *hoi huioi tou theou* ‘‘the sons of God’’ in Genesis 6:2. Translation is already taking us far from the implication of the original conception of superhuman men (e.g., Nimrod) and mythological beings *(Gabr-i-’el, miy-ka-’el, rafa’-’el,* and *Śaṭan). Gabr-i-’el* is the *ẹl-ẹ́-gbara* (Amharic *gebre)* of *’$^{\varepsilon}$l.* Those who know the ordinary meaning of Greek *angeloi* know that it means only ‘‘messengers,’’ just as Hebrew *mal$^{e}$'ak-iym* means "messengers" ordinarily. But when mythical thinking enters into it, Greek *angeloi* and Hebrew *ma-l$^{e}$'ak-iym* are rendered into English as *angels*. Ordinarily Hebrew *ma-l$^{e}$'ak* should be Hausa *ma-aiki* "messenger" (not *màlékà,* which is a late Islamic loan word from Arabic *malaa'ika* "angels") and Yoruba *ukọ̀/ikọ̀* "emissary."

The Jews who translated the Hebrew Bible (Old Testament) into Greek in Alexandria avoided the mythology of *b$^{e}$n-ey ha-'$^{ε}$loh-iym* in Genesis 6:1 and Job 1:6 but gave us another myth—that of angels of God who are not *b$^{e}$n-ey ha-'$^{ε}$loh-iym:*

| | Hebrew Original | Greek Septuagint | New Testament |
|---|---|---|---|
| Genesis 6:1 | *b$^{e}$n-ey ha-'$^{ε}$loy-iym* | *hoi huioi tou theou* | |
| Job 1:6 | *b$^{e}$n-ey ha-'$^{ε}$loh-iym* | *hoi angeloi tou theou* | |
| Psalm 8:6 | *'$^{ε}$loh-iym* | *angelous* | Hebrews 2:7 |
| Psalm 8:4a | *'$^{ε}$no$^{w}$š* | *anthropos* | Hebrews 2:6 |
| Psalm 8:4b | *bεn 'adam* | *huios anthropou* | |

Note the following changes:

*i)* The plural *-iym* in Hebrew *'$^{ε}$loh-iym* is not reflected in Greek *theou.* Monotheism is responsible for such a change.

*ii)* The mythological suggestion that the "(spiritual) lords" have sons is unacceptable to the Jewish translators of the Septuagint: "sons of the (spiritual) lords" becomes "angels of God" in Job 1:6. And yet "lords" in Psalm 8:6 also becomes "angels." Mythology in the Bible embarrassed the orthodoxy of Jewish leaders even in the second century B.C. They therefore passed on both the lords and the sons of the lords as the same thing—angels, the characteristic mythological beings of monotheism.

*iii)* If *'$^{ε}$loah* "God" (Yoruba *Olúwa* "lord") occurs in the plural *'$^{ε}$loh-iym,* the Jewish translators decided that it must refer to angels as divine beings (Ps. 8:6). There could not be a plurality of gods.

*iv)* The Septuagint translators lost the distinction between *'$^{ε}$no$^{w}$š* and *'adam,* and equated the son with the father.

Since mythology attempts to penetrate into what things were like *me-'o$^{w}$lam* "from eternity," from the very beginning of existence, the part of the Bible that shows the myth content most is Genesis 1–11.

There is a difference between saying that Genesis 1–11 *contains* myths and saying that Genesis 1–11 *is* myth. Genesis 1–11 *uses* ancient Near Eastern myths of polydaemonism for the theological purposes of monotheism. It is theology, not mythology. The means is not the end. The writers of 1 Samuel, 2 Samuel, 1 Kings, and 2 Kings use *history* (historical documents—the Chronicles of the Kings of Judah, the Chronicles of the Kings of Israel) to write theology, and the writers of Joshua and Judges use *legend* (the Book of the Wars of Yahweh) and *heroic saga* (the narrative poems in the Book of Yashar) to write theology.

To write theology we must use an instrument. If we use philosophy we get philosophical theology (e.g., the book of Proverbs, Ecclesiastes, and Job). If we use history we get historical theology. If we use traditional mythology we get the type of theological writing we have in Genesis 1–11.

The purpose of theology is not to banish mythology, for that cannot be done once and for all as long as human beings are mythmakers. Most demythologizing ends in remythologizing. Thus centuries after Moses announced to the Hebrews who had recently left polydaemonic Egypt that their god(s) was a single YHWH, the early Christians said that God was a triune God, a statement that is repugnant to monotheism (e.g., Islam) except it be clarified. It is the purpose of theology to clarify the meaning of myths. The right question to ask about a myth is not "Is it accurate?" but "What does it mean?"

To understand theology fully, the student is encouraged to read *relevant* mythology. The myths that are traditionally considered relevant are Near Eastern myths, particularly Babylonian. Cyrus Gordon has shown in *Before the Bible* that Greek myths are also relevant. We now say that African myths are very relevant because the Hebrew language is not only a Semitic language (related to Akkadian, Aramaic, Ugaritic, Arabic, Ge'ez, and Amharic) but also a Hamito-Semitic language (related on a wider scale and at a deeper level in time to Ancient Egyptian, Berber, Kushitic, and Chadic). That is, four of the five branches of the Hamito-Semitic family as currently accepted are located in Africa (see map on p. 35). What we are contributing is to expose the "extremely remote relationship between the Niger-Congo and Hamitic families as a whole" which J. H. Greenberg admitted.[5]

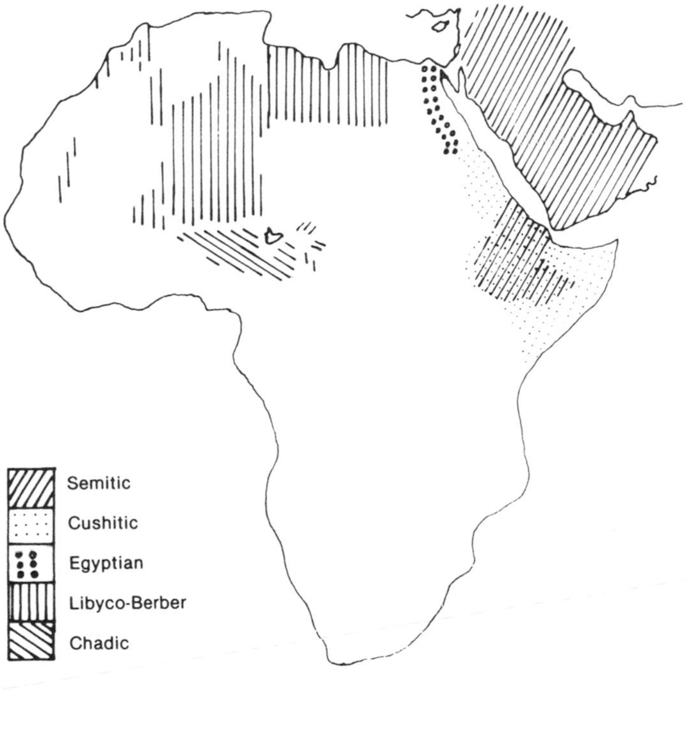


The Hamito-Semitic Language Area

# 4

# The Paradise in Eden

## "The Garden of Eden"

What we know from the English versions of the Bible as "the garden of Eden" is in the Hebrew original *gan* $b^e$*-‘edɛn*, where Hebrew *gan* "garden" is Hausa *gona* "farm" and Yoruba *ẹ-gan* "virgin forest, black loamy soil." The Hebrew $b^e$ "in" (i.e., in a place) is reflected in Middle Egyptian *bw* "place," Bantu *bu/bo* "place" (e.g., *Bu-ganda* "place of the *Ba-ganda*"; *Bu-rundi* "place of the *Ba-rundi*"; *Bo-tswana* "place of the *Ba-tswana*"; Ijẹbu Yoruba *u-bo* "place" (*ubo-k-úbo* "any place," i.e., anywhere), Koine Yoruba *i-bi* and Igbo *e-be* "place." The Hebrew *‘edɛn* "delight" is Yoruba *a-dùn* "delight, enjoyment." Hence Hebrew *ma-*$^{‘a}$*dan-iym* "delicacies": Yoruba *mù-dùn-mú-dùn* "sweet repast."

That Hebrew *‘edɛn* is "delight" is the traditional interpretation. E. A. Speiser has suggested an alternative: Hebrew *‘edɛn*: Assyrian *edinu* "plain," which is matched by Yoruba *ọ̀dàn* "grassland." The Hebrews would find such a plain not in Palestine but in Mesopotamia, which is east of Palestine. This would explain *miq-qɛdɛm* "in the east."[1] Note that the river that flowed out of *‘edɛn* divided into four rivers, two of which are *Ḥiddɛqɛl* (Tigris), which flows east from Assyria, and $P^e$*raṭ* (Eu-phrat-es). Further support for this etymology of *‘edɛn* may be found in Genesis 11:2: "When men struck camp and migrated *miq-qɛdɛm* ('from the east'), they found a *biq*$^e$*‘-ah* in *’ɛrɛṣ šin*$^e$*‘ar*. . . ."

Hebrew *biq<sup>e</sup>'-ah* "plain" is Yoruba *kpákpá* "grass field." (Compare the underlying Hebrew verb *baqa'* "to hatch, to break," and Yoruba *kpa* "to hatch.") We know that Yoruba *kpákpá* "flat grass field" is a synonym for Yoruba *ọ̀dàn* "grassland." The modern philological suggestion that Hebrew *'edɛn* means "plain" helps us to locate the possible area *miq-qɛdɛm* "in the east" in the same area as the *biq<sup>e</sup>'ah* of Genesis 11:2, which is also *miq-qɛdɛm* "in the east." The land of Shinar (*'ɛrɛṣ šin<sup>e</sup>'ar*) is definitely Mesopotamia.

This leads our thoughts along the lines of geography, but the writer of Genesis 2 wanted to lead our thoughts along the lines of theology—philosophy with its ethical corollaries. Hence he preferred the traditional etymology, which says that Hebrew *'edɛn* means "delight."

Note that folk etymology is not interested in philological accuracy. For instance, the preposition *b<sup>e</sup>-* "in" alone is sufficient to help a philologist, particularly when the preposition of place is followed by a noun of direction, *miq-qɛdɛm* "from/in the east." A plain can be located in the east (of Palestine); delight does not have a geographical location.

This is one of the causes of the differences between the traditional interpretations of Genesis 1–11 and the modern philological interpretations. The philological interpretations are more accurate—and accuracy is an academic (intellectual) judgment. It is not a theological assessment. In academics (e.g., mathematics) we speak of accuracy or inaccuracy. In theology (e.g., poetry) we are not interested in accuracy for its own sake. Instead the poet takes poetic license and yet achieves beauty.

What should we use Bible study for—for ethics (philosophy, theology) or for philology (archeology, linguistics, prehistory)? Is it an either/or problem or a both/and situation? Material for both is in the Bible. What happens is that students of the Bible notice *(i)* what interests them, and *(ii)* what they are academically equipped to discover.

Concerning *(ii)* we must note that the Bible is one of the few books in the world that is read to, or read by, people from the age of five until the age of one hundred, by the farmer and by the Hamito-Semitic linguist. All these people tend to argue with each other about the meaning of a passage. They should realize that the meaning of a passage of Scripture depends on *(i)* what interests the reader; *(ii)* how many years the reader has been pondering the passage; and *(iii)* what life-experiences the reader has to bring to life words and phrases in the passage.

Two such life-experiences are travel (geographical and historical studies offer a substitute for this) and deep knowledge of the original language in which the passage was written (there is no substitute for this).

Persons who read Genesis in the Hebrew original observe nuances that are lost on those who read it in translation. And those who know not only Hebrew but also related languages know that the Hebrew noun *gan* "garden" is from the verbal root *ganan* "to fence around," and so is related to the other Hebrew noun *gann-ah* (: Yoruba *ì-gànná* "wall fencing in a yard"), which is reflected in Arabic as *jannah*, the symbol in the Qur'an for *'al jannah* (» Hausa » Yoruba *àlùjọ́nnà* "paradise" [heaven]).

The *gan* that *YHWH 'ᵋloh-iym* "planted" (actually Hebrew *naṭa'*: Yoruba *ta* in *ta ọgbà* "erect a fence to protect a garden"; Jukun *ta* "plant"—not "sow") is *miq-qɛdɛm* "in the east," because the Hebrews knew of such luxuries as game parks and pleasure gardens not in Canaan but in the east—the Mesopotamian area. When the Persian kings permitted the Jewish exiles to return to rebuild Jerusalem, Nehemiah requested from King Artaxerxes a letter for Asaph:

> *šomer hap-parᵉdes 'ᵃšɛr lam-mɛlɛk.*
>
> that he may supply me with *ᶜᵉṣ-iym* for the repairs on the gates of the temple [Neh. 2:8a].

When Nehemiah began his work of reconstruction in Jerusalem one of the jobs he tackled was that "he built the wall of the Pool of Shelah next to *gan ham-mɛlɛk*" (Neh. 3:15).

In Hebrew, then, a *gan* was not a farm. When inside a city, it was a garden. David and Solomon had provided themselves with such a *gan* in Jerusalem. When in the countryside it was not a jungle but a *parᵉdes* "a forest reserve and a game park" owned by a king or a magnate who put in charge a *šomer* "a keeper." That esthete and eclectic, Ecclesiastes, said in chapter 2:4–6 that when he went all-out for pomp and grand projects, he built for himself houses, planted (*nṭ'*) vineyards, and constructed *gann-o*$^{w}$*t* and *par*$^{e}$*des-iym*, and he planted (*nṭ'*) in them *'eṣ kol p*$^{e}$*riy* "the tree of every fruit." He made a pool of water from which *l*$^{e}$*-ha-š*$^{e}$*q-o*$^{w}$*t* "to water" the *ya'ar* "forest" of growing trees. Thus YHWH *'*$^{ɛ}$*loh-iym* put *ha-'adam* in the *gan* he had fenced round in *'edɛn*

> *l*$^{e}$*-'ab*$^{e}$*d-ah u*$^{w}$*-l*$^{e}$*-šom*$^{e}$*r-ah.*
>
> to till it and to watch it [Gen. 2:15b].

As there were *'eṣ-iym* "trees" (Igbo *osisi*; Ewe *tso*) in the *par*$^{e}$*des* of the king of Persia fit for making the door of the temple in Jerusalem, so there were in the *gan* in *'edɛn* all sorts of *'eṣ-iym*. As in any animal park or forest reserve, we expect notices to be put up: "All the trees of the *gan* you are free to eat. But from the tree of ——— you may not eat of it. For on the day you eat of it, you will. . . ." Life in Eden, then, was pleasurably horticultural—not laboriously agricultural as it became after the expulsion of *'adam* and *Ḥawwah* from the *gan* in *'edɛn*. It was a luxurious pastime, not a subsistence necessity. *'Adam* and *Ḥawwah* did not "die" when they trespassed in the *gan* in *'edɛn* by transgressing the bounds set by the owner of the *gan*.

But "life" outside *'al jann-ah* has been such that we *b*$^{e}$*n-ey ha-'adam* now ask:

> What is this life if, full of care,
> We have no time to stand and stare?

To experience the life of *'edɛn* overworked Americans take a vacation and go to Hawaii, whose praises they sing as "the isle of Paradise." To experience such a life, people engage not in work but in recreation. To ensure that urbanization and civilization do not push out such a life entirely, Hyde Park is preserved in the midst of London and the housewife plants flowers in pots on the balcony of the tenth-floor flat where her family live enclosed in concrete.

What person does not carry in his or her heart a memory of Paradise Lost? What people do not strive for Paradise Regained through the arts of *Ḥanoʷk* and *Tuʷbal Qayin*? Yet no people ever opt for a return to *‘edɛn*, since the door is barred for a return to the life of the noble savage—naked and yet not ashamed. Instead a *gan* is designed into the *urbs* of the future dream:

> So in the Spirit he carried me away to a great high mountain, and showed me the holy city of Jerusalem coming down out of heaven from God. . . . The city was built as a square, and was as wide as it was long. . . . The streets of the city were of pure gold, like translucent glass [Rev. 21:10, 16, 21].

In that vision in the last book of the New Testament, John the Apocalyptist has saved us from the need to sentimentalize *gan bᵉ-‘edɛn* by equating *parᵉdes* with the kingdom of God. Such an equation is a myth. John demythologized the myth that says that rural life is godly and city life is devilish by changing the imagery of the kingdom of God. A king lives in the capital of his kingdom:

> I saw no temple in the city; for its temple was YHWH *’ᵋloh-iym ṣᵉba’-oʷt* and the Lamb. The city had no need of sun or moon. . . .
>
> Then he showed me the river of the water of life, sparkling like crystal, flowing from the throne of God and of the Lamb down the middle of the city’s street. On either side of the river stood a tree of life, which yields twelve crops of fruit, one for each month of the year . . . [Rev. 21:22–23; 22:1–2].

What are we praying for: Paradise Regained or the City of God? The beautiful Africa of the past before the Europeans came to spoil the world and the missionaries came to turn men into women? Or are we prepared to theologize what happened in history and say: “*YHWH ’ᵋloh-iym* made tunics of skins for Adam and his wife and clothed them.” One is sentimental romanticism; the other is realistic acceptance of those facts in our personal and social past that it is not in our power to change. The partition of Africa may be an imperialist sin, but we have not reversed the partition lines after independence. Instead we have constitutionalized the partition in the O.A.U. charter, which maintains the boundaries as they were at independence. No going back to the prepartition boundaries.

If an unmarried girl of sixteen gets pregnant, we are scandalized by the sin, but when the "illegitimate child" arrives we do not strangle it and make the mother a maiden again. Nor do we say the child is a child of the devil. We bring it up as a child of God and say, theologically, "God made for Adam and his wife tunics of skin and clothed them."

*'Adam* was expelled from horticulture to agriculture, and his first son took after him:

> *Qayin* was *'ɛbɛd 'adam-ah.*
>
> Cain was a slave of the soil [Gen. 4:2].

Hebrew *Qayin* (Cain) is Arabic *qayn* "smith." My own research in the African side of the Hamito-Semitic (Afro-Asiatic) family of languages enables me to extend this: the occupation of *Qayin* in Genesis 4:1–2 should be studied together with the occupation of *Tu$^w$bal Qayin* (Tubal Cain) in Genesis 4:22. And with the culture-history implications of the following cognates:

| | | |
|---|---|---|
| Arabic | *quyun* | "smith(s)" |
| Fọn | *Gún* | "*vodũ* of blacksmiths" (Bini *O-gun*) |
| Yoruba | *Ò-gún* | "*òrìṣà* of blacksmiths" (Bini *O-gun*) |
| Hahm (Jaba) | *Kuno* | "The evil spirit who built the iron furnaces" |
| Hausa | *ma-qeri* | "blacksmith" |
| Fọn | *gun* | "iron" (Gɛn *gã*; Aja *gã*; Ewe *gã*) |

Domestication of animals (goats, sheep, cattle, etc.) did not bring back the bliss of Eden. In fact its first practitioner was named *Hɛbɛl*, the word translated as "vanity" in Ecclesiastes. In any case early death prevented *Hɛbɛl* from leaving descendants: the history of civilization is not the history of shepherds as the Hamitic hypothesis suggests: *Hɛbɛl* had no son, no descendants. His line was cut off by the might of the farmer from whose line came the discovery of iron by *Tu$^w$bal Qayin* (Yoruba *Ò-gún*) and the building of cities (*Ḥano$^w$k: Nok*).[2]

## The River(s) That Flowed out of *'Edεn*

> A *nahar* [river] flowed out of *'Edεn* to *ha-š̌*$^{e}$*q-o*$^{w}$*t* [water] the *gan*. From the *gan* it parted into four [streams]. The name of one is *Piyš̌-o*$^{w}$*n*: it flows round all the land of *Ḥawiylah* in which is gold. . . . The name of the second *nahar* is *Giyḥ-o*$^{w}$*n*. This is the river which flows round all the land of *Ku*$^{w}$*š̌*. The name of the third *nahar* is *Ḥiddεqεl*. It flows east of *'Aš̌š̌u*$^{w}$*r*. And the fourth *nahar* is *P*$^{e}$*raṭ* [Gen. 2:10–14].

The *nahar* named *P*$^{e}$*raṭ* was known by the Greeks as *Eu-phrat-es* "good [river] *P*$^{e}$*raṭ*."

The names of big rivers frequently mean simply "river." Hence Semitic *nhr* was used as the word "Nile" to name the river that the Egyptians called *itrw* (see Nembe Ijọ *tọrụ* "river"). The *nahar* of Egypt is the Nile (of Egypt). This is why there is a White Nile and a Blue Nile. Each is a *nahar* in its own right.

Where is the *nahar P*$^{e}$*raṭ*? Babylonia, in one word. More exactly it flows from north Syria in the west in a southeasterly direction through Babylonia into the sea in the Gulf of Aden. North of it flows the *nahar Ḥiddεqεl* in the same direction, passing therefore through Assyria (*'Aš̌š̌u*$^{w}$*r*). It is the Tigris. Turn to Daniel 10:4 and you will not be surprised that Daniel, living as he was in Babylon until Cyrus the Persian overtook Babylon, was standing on the bank of the great *nahar*, that is, the *Ḥiddεqεl*.

The geographical setting of *'Edεn* (Assyrian *edinu* "plain"; Yoruba *ọ̀dàn* "flat grassland") is therefore the *biq*$^{e}$*'-ah* (: Yoruba *kpákpá*) of Mesopotamia—the land between (two) rivers. For *Ḥawiylah* borders Babylonia in the northeastern half of the fertile crescent (it is mentioned in Gen. 10:7 as one of the sons of Kush). The land benefited from the floods of the *Ḥiddεqεl* and the *P*$^{e}$*raṭ* just as Egypt, the southwestern half, benefited from the floods of the Nile.

It seems that the floods of the Mesopotamian rivers brought not only fertile loam but sometimes disastrous overflowing. It is from this area that the myth of universal flood in primeval times originated. The Yahwist writer in Genesis 2 took over the myth to illustrate a point: the natural disaster that human beings bring upon themselves by their own sin. This is not science (not natural history); it is religion (theologizing).

Which is the *nahar Giyḥoʷn* that flows around all the land of *Kuʷš*? *Kuʷš* is the land of the blacks south of Egypt (the land the Greeks called *Aithiopias*). The inclusion of such a river as one of the four branches of the river that flows out of Eden makes *'Edɛn* a place that never was, for we have here a geographical impossibility. We know that before the Age of Exploration and the subsequent detailed mapping of the world there was much vagueness about the sources and the mouths of famous rivers (e.g., the Nile and the *Kwara*). Such vagueness may account for the suggestion that a river of the land of *Kuʷš* has a common source with the Tigris and the *Eu-phrat-es*. Precise geographical knowledge dismisses this as ancient myth, just as the explorations of Mungo Park and the Lander brothers showed to Europeans that the *Kwara* does not flow into the Nile.

It is no use mounting an expedition to discover *'Edɛn* or Mount Ararat. It is of no religious use. It may satisfy academic curiosity, but academics are not the concern of religion. As far as religion is concerned, the *nahar Pᵉraṭ* may be the *Volta* in Ewe land, and the *Giyḥ-oʷn* may be the river *Ògùn* in Abẹokuta. This does not change the theology a jot. It is like Jesus saying to people who may want to go in a spacecraft in search of the kingdom of God: "The kingdom of God is within you."

# 5

# The Tree of Life or the Tree of Knowledge?

These metaphysics of magicians
And necromantic books are heavenly;
Ay, these are those that Faustus most desires.
What a world of profit and delight, . . .
A sound magician is a mighty god:
Here, Faustus, try thy brains to gain a deity.

Christopher Marlowe, *Dr. Faustus*

Has the reader ever noticed that when God commanded Adam not to eat of the fruit of the tree of the knowledge of good and evil, he did not prohibit the eating of fruit from the tree of life? God was silent about that. The tree of life was included in all the other trees from which Adam was free to eat. But did Adam or *Ḥawwah* try the tree of life? The answer is No.

Why? we may ask. Because human beings in their folly choose by attractive appearance. The tree of life was not distinguished by beauty. On the contrary, the fruit of the tree of the knowledge of good and evil was good for eating (Hebrew *ṭo*$^{w}$*b* "good": Yoruba *tóbi* "big") and it was beautiful to the eyes (Hebrew *ta-*$^{'a}$*wah* "beautiful": Yoruba *ẹwà* "beauty") and desirable as a means of making one wise (Hebrew *nɛ-ḥ*$^{e}$*mad* "praised everywhere") (Gen. 3:6).

Foolishly, human beings tend to choose by outward appearances. It was for this that Shakespeare told the story of the three caskets in *The Merchant of Venice*—one of gold, one of silver, one of lead. It was for this that the Yoruba told the story of the tree whose fruits were shouting *ká mi, kà mi, ká mi* ("pluck me, pluck me, pluck me"), while the fruits of another tree were still like waters that run deep.

## The Knowledge of Good and Evil

Let us examine the symbol of this tree. It is not merely the tree of knowledge. If it had been simply the tree of the knowledge of good, it would have presented no problem. If it had been simply the tree of the knowledge of evil, no one would have chosen of its fruit. But it was not a simple tree: it was a tree of the knowledge of good and evil. Both good and evil. This choice of the fruits of a tree that is seen (appears) to be *nε-ḥ$^{e}$mad l$^{e}$-ha-s$^{e}$kiyl* "of great reputation for making one wise" (Gen. 3:6) reveals a basic error of judgment in human nature, which this symbol was constructed to lay bare.

Let us turn to the picture of the servant of Yahweh in Isaiah 52:13:

> *hinneh ya-s$^{e}$kiyl 'ab$^{e}$d-iy. . . .*
>
> Behold, my servant shall possess knowledge. . . .

But this servant of Yahweh was neither beautiful nor desirable to behold:

> He had neither *to'ar* nor *hadar*
> for us to want to look at him;
> And *lo' ma-r$^{e}$'εh w$^{e}$-nε-ḥ$^{e}$m$^{e}$d-e-hu$^{w}$* [Isa. 53:2b].

The meaning of this passage should be checked from the various versions. The tree of the knowledge of good and evil was *nε-ḥ$^{e}$mad l$^{e}$-ha-s$^{e}$kiyl* "reputed to be able to make one learned." As for the servant of Yahweh, public opinion rated him low in the matter of wisdom and skill. But in spite of his lack of external attractiveness, Yahweh chose him to be his servant and declared: "My servant shall *śkl.*"

We know from Isaiah 49:3 that the servant of Yahweh is a personification of Israel, chosen to be the people of God even though it was not a famous nation. God does not choose as human beings choose; human beings tend to choose the beautiful; God chose the one without beauty. When the tree of life stood available in the *gan* in *'edɛn* man ignored it and strove against divine prohibition to taste of the fruit of another tree—the beautiful tree, the tree praised to the skies in popular opinion.

### *Naked and Not Ashamed*

The fruit of this beautiful tree—the forbidden fruit—is not sexual intercourse, as some people have suggested. When Adam and his wife were naked, they were not ashamed (Gen. 2:25), for it is not a shameful thing for a man and his wife to be naked together.

And in early times (i.e., in primitive times), nakedness was not considered a thing of shame in the warm climates of Africa. Not for men and not for maidens. Among the Dinka of the Sudan men went naked. Zulu men also went naked. Men and women among the Birom of Jos Plateau in Nigeria went naked until the 1940s. They despised those who wore clothes; for they said that they must be hiding something shameful or they would not be covering up. Until today, if you see a girl or woman in Ewe land with a white wrapper that does not cover her breasts, you know that she is a priestess—not a topless model. For nakedness used to be a sign of purity—of a transparent life.

It is this primitive state of innocence that Genesis is picturing for us—when men wore no clothes and yet were not ashamed, when maidens went bare-breasted and yet were not ashamed. In fact, to start covering up before marriage made a girl suspect. What is she ashamed of? Has she done something to be ashamed of? Children were expected to go naked—and you were a child until puberty rites for girls and circumcision at initiation for boys.

### *The Opening of the Eyes*

No one was ashamed of nakedness until civilized men who had lost the childhood innocence of primitive peoples began to open the eyes of the world. Note that the Yoruba word for a civilized person is *ọ̀làjú (ọ̀-là-jú* "the one whose eyes have been opened"). The temptation of the serpent, then, is the temptation of civilization for primitive peoples. For the Yoruba, examples of *ọ̀làjú* are found in prostitutes. Prostitutes are not found among naked tribes.

Are we modern civilized peoples happier than our primitive ancestors? Genesis answers with a symbolic story: men and women lived naked when they were living in

*gan bᵉ-'edɛn* "the garden in Eden" (Hebrew Bible—Genesis)
*paradeisos en Eden* "paradise in Eden" (Greek version—Septuagint)
*-junna-tᵘ fi 'adᵉn-in* "the garden (paradise) in Eden" (Arabic version).

Thus medieval European artists symbolized cherubs as naked babies. Hebrew *keruʷb* is, in fact, Yoruba *ò-gìrìkpá* "stalwart." In Greek mythology, it is *grups* (» English *griffon*).

What is the origin of clothing among human beings? The answer of Genesis is plain. Why, then, did God make garments of animal hide for Adam and *Ḥawwah* and clothe them? This question is like asking, "Why did Moses ask the Jewish men who wanted to divorce their wives to give them a note of divorce?"

We see here something about the concept "God": *Vox populi, vox dei.* Adam and *Ḥawwah* wanted clothes: they sewed fig leaves together and made for themselves aprons, as the Birom did until the 1940s. Technological advance helped them to improve on this by giving them garments of animal hide. If originally the wearing of clothes came because *ha-'adam* and *Ḥawwah* had done a deed of shame, why did they not repent and go back to the state of nakedness? It is difficult to find any people who have done this. The wearing of clothes persists, and it is rationalized as good. In fact, it is said that God provided clothing.

Do we still believe that knowledge is good and evil? Consider electronics (telephone, tape recorders, and bugging devices). Consider electricity (light, power, electrocution). Consider atomic research (atomic energy and atomic bombs). Consider pharmacy and pharmacology (medicines and poisons). Knowledge—it is now accepted—is amoral, neither moral nor immoral because it is capable of being both. Semitic languages signify this awareness in the connotations of the roots:

| | *‘-l-m* | *‘-r-m* |
|---|---|---|
| HEBREW | *‘alam,* ‘‘conceal’’ | *‘aru$^{w}$m* ‘‘cunning’’ (Gen. 3:1a) |
| | *ta-‘$^{a}$lu$^{w}$m-ah* ‘‘secret’’ | *‘ar$^{e}$m-ah,* ‘‘craftiness’’ |
| | *‘o$^{w}$lam* ‘‘unknown past,’’ ‘‘unknown future’’ | |
| ARABIC | *‘ilm* ‘‘(secret) knowledge’’ | |
| | *mu-‘aliym,* ‘‘master of (secret) knowledge’’ | *‘aru$^{w}$m,* ‘‘be ill-natured’’ |
| | *‘aalam,* ‘‘cosmos’’ | |

This double potential of all knowledge, not only witchcraft, is symbolized in the tree of the knowledge of good and evil—attractive yet able to deprive the learned of the blissful life of the ignorant.

Consider these two excerpts from W. B. Anderson in *The Church in East Africa:*

> . . . Merensky, the head of the Berlin Society, prophesied an eclipse on 15 November 1891. The prophecy was fulfilled but this only proved to the Mbasi that the missionaries were dangerous. When the rains failed to come, the Mbasi priest blamed the Berlin Mission, ordering that the missionaries should be killed.[1]

> . . . [Mackay] spoke most strongly against the *lubaale* (hero-gods) and the charms associated with them which the people wore. He threw a *lubaale* charm on the fire once. The Baganda ran away horrified, or looked on thunderstruck. When Mackay did not fall down and die, some said, ‘‘You are a god.’’ Others said, ‘‘You are a devil.’’[2]

Macbeth got himself entangled in the equivocation of the fiend that lies like truth. Knowledge—science—is equivocal. And yet what primitive peoples are not bewitched by the technological fruits of science (airplanes, radio, cinema and television, firearms)? Demonstrate these before any primitive tribes and they will be enticed out of Eden before they know it. That is the way of human beings.

## Man and the God(s)

YHWH *’$^{\varepsilon}$loh-iym* said (Gen. 3:22), ‘‘Behold, the Adam has become like one of us—able to know good and evil.’’ Man is like the gods. And in Genesis 1:26 *’$^{\varepsilon}$loh-iym* said: ‘‘Let us make Adam in our own shape—to resemble us. . . .’’ Man is like the gods.

Note what is stated in Psalm 8 in answer to the question put to God:

| | |
|---|---|
| What is *’$^{\varepsilon}$no$^{w}$š . . .?* | (Yoruba *Kí ni ènìy-àn?)* |
| What is *b$^{\varepsilon}$n ’adam . . .?* | (Yoruba *Kí ni ọmọ Ádámọ̀?)* |

The answer given in verse 6 is:

> You have made him in such a way that what he lacks of the qualities of *’$^{\varepsilon}$loh-iym* is little.
> You have crowned him with *kabo$^{w}$d* and *hadar*.

That *kabo$^{w}$d* ‘‘glory/glare’’ is an attribute of God and not just of angels can be seen in Isaiah 42:8 and 13:

> *’an-iy YHWH . . . u$^{w}$-k$^{e}$bo$^{w}$d-iy l$^{e}$-’aḥer lo’ ’ɛt-ten u$^{w}$-t$^{e}$-hillat-iy lap-p$^{e}$siyl-iym.*
> *ya-siym-u$^{w}$ la-YHWH kabo$^{w}$d u$^{w}$-t$^{e}$-hillat-o$^{w}$.*

> I am YHWH . . . and my *kabo$^{w}$d* I do not give to another; nor [do I give] my praise to idols [vs. 8].
> Give to YHWH the *kabo$^{w}$d* and praise due to him [vs. 13].

And *hadar* (: Yoruba *dára;* Swahili *u-zuri* ‘‘good, beautiful’’) is ‘‘splendor, majesty.’’

*’$^{\varepsilon}$no$^{w}$š* (: Igbo *onye* ‘‘person’’: Arabic *’in$^{e}$s-aan* ‘‘human being’’; Yoruba *ènìy-àn* ‘‘human being’’) is little less than *’$^{\varepsilon}$loh-iym* ‘‘(spiritual) lords’’ in immortality. When he had full opportunity to eat of the fruit of the tree of life in the garden of Eden, he did

not. He gained the knowledge of everything but lost life. God barred to him the gate to the tree of *ìyè*.

In every other respect, *bɛn ha-'adam* is like *bɛn ha-'ᵋloh-iym*. In any situation where people consider it blasphemy that a man should claim to be *bɛn ha-'ᵋloh-iym,* the man need not worry. He merely needs to call himself *bɛn ha-'adam*. Those who are ignorant of the fact that *bɛn ha-'adam* is almost equivalent to *bɛn ha-'ᵋloh-iym* will be fooled. And Jesus liked to fool wicked people who look and look but do not see, and listen and listen but do not hear. The title *bɛn ha-'adam* "son of *'adam*" is thus one of the ways by which Jesus concealed his consciousness that he was *bɛn ha-'ᵋloh-iym*. Jesus therefore did not consider it degrading to call himself *bɛn ha-'adam* "the son of *'adam*"—a phrase which in Psalm 8 occurs in synonymous parallelism with the word *'ɛnoʷš* "man."

Some people do not like human beings to be considered too much like *'ᵋloh-iym,* "(spiritual) lords." In translating Psalm 8:6 they say: "You have made him a little less than angels," when the original clearly says "a little less than *'ᵋloh-iym.*" They are embarrassed because Hebrew *'ᵋloh-iym,* masculine plural of *'ᵋloah* (: Yoruba *Olúwa* "lord"[3]) is, according to Hebrew thinking, "god(s)"—divine beings.

They show the same unwillingness to accept what *Ḥawwah* said in Genesis 4:1 when she gave birth to *Qayin:*

*qan-iy-tiy 'iyš 'ᵋt YHWH.*

I have created a man—a YHWH.

That is—a man, particularly a blacksmith, is a YHWH, a spiritual being. See Fọn *Yɛhwe*, Ewe *Yèvè* "spirit," and Gun *Yihwe Yɛhwe* "God." They avoid this identification of *'iyš* and YHWH by translating the passage: "I have acquired a man with the help of YHWH."

Where do they get "with the help of" in the original Hebrew?[4] Hebrew *'ɛt* is either the preposition "with" (: Yoruba *àti* "with"; Chichewa *ndi* "and"; Hausa *da)* or the particle that introduces the direct object. Those versions have understood it to be the first. I cannot see any reason for this but that they think the other possibility blasphemous. "How can an *'iyš* be a YHWH?" they ask. When Ecclesiastes said *qan-iy-tiy 'abad-iym uʷ-šefaḥoʷt*

(2:7a) he was using the same verb *qanah (i)* "to buy, to acquire," *(ii)* "to fabricate, to create."

*YHWH**

Actually YHWH is not a Hebrew word, as Robert H. Pfeiffer has pointed out. The word *pɛsaḥ,* erroneously interpreted as "passover," is also cited by Pfeiffer: "Since Hebrew is demonstrably the language of Canaan (Is. 19:18) before it was the language of Israel, the language of the Israelites in the desert in the time of Moses is unknown except for two words which are not Hebrew: *pɛsaḥ* (passover) and Yahweh (Jehovah)."[5] In fact, *pɛsaḥ* is cognate with Twi *a-fašɛ* "festival"—main festival, and YHWH is a reflex of Fọn *Yɛhwe* "Spirit," a synonym of Fọn *vodũ.* A man is definitely a spirit: *ru$^{w}$aḥ '$^{\varepsilon}$loh-iym* is in his nostrils. If you bought a golden earring you would say you had acquired a thing; if you gave birth to a child, you could say, as *Ḥawwah* said: "I have acquired a man—a spirit being." Did God not say of men in Scripture:

"Ye are *'$^{\varepsilon}$loh-iym*—
all sons of *'ɛl$^{e}$y-o$^{w}$n"* [Ps. 82:6]?

You are lords—
all sons of *Ẹnyọn.*[6]

And Jesus: "Be ye perfect, even as your father in heaven is perfect" (Mt. 5:28). How can our father be God and we not be divine, if we are legitimate children?

If *Ḥawwah* says that her son *Qayin* (:Yoruba *Ògún)* is a *Yɛhwe* "a divine spirit," Psalm 29 says that the voice of YHWH is *Kalu,* the *alúsi* "divine being" of thunder among the Igbo:

The *qo$^{w}$l* ["thunder"] of YHWH is [heard] upon the flooded waters
*'el* of *kabo$^{w}$d* causes thunder. . . .
The *qo$^{w}$l* of YHWH is in *ike*
The *qo$^{w}$l* of YHWH is in majestic splendor
The *qo$^{w}$l* of YHWH breaks the cedars—

*See also Appendix, section II, "YHWH."

> YHWH causes the cedars of Lebanon to be broken. . . .
> The *qo$^{w}$l* of YHWH makes the lightning flash. . . .

*Qayin* is *Ògún*—an *òrìṣà* in Yoruba belief (note: *Ènìyàn ni í d' òrìṣà,* "it is *'anaš-iym* ['human beings'] who become *ri'š-on-iym*" ["ancestral spirits"]); *qo$^{w}$l YHWH* is *Kalu*—an *alúsi* in Igbo belief. That is a *Yεhwe*. Roberto Pazzi writes: "On appelle F[ọn]: *Yεhwè*/E[we]: *Yèvè* (Esprit bas) la Puissance de la Foudre (et celle de l'Arc en Ciel)."[7]

Do not forget that even Moses, who first learned about the divine "name" YHWH in Midian, left us the impression that YHWH was lightning whose voice was thunder:

> Moses went up Mount Sinai and a cloud covered it. *K$^{e}$bo$^{w}$d YHWH* ["the dazzling light of the Lord's presence," T.E.V.] came down on the mountain. To the Israelites the light looked like a fire burning on top of the mountain [Exod. 24:15–17].
>
> Moses was speaking and *ha-'$^{\varepsilon}$loh-iym* was answering him with *Kalu* [Exod. 19:19b].[8]

The Yoruba say that

*Ní 'jọ́ Ọgún ń t' orí òkè bọ̀*
*Aṣọ iná l' ó fi bo 'ra*
*Ẹ̀wù ẹ̀jẹ̀ l' ó wọ̀.*

On the day *Ògún* was coming from the top of the mountain,
It was with fire he covered himself;
It was clothes of blood he wore.

Elijah expected this manifestation of YHWH when he ran from the persecution of Jezebel to complain on Mount Horeb. But he learned a new lesson: YHWH was not in the lightning; YHWH was not in the thunder; YHWH was in a still small voice. Was this conscience?

# 6

# Noah and the Ark

## Noah and *Ma-no*ʷ*aḥ*

Was it that Noah found *ḥen* (: Yoruba *àánú*; "mercy, grace") in the eyes of YHWH (Gen. 6:8b) or was he spared because he was *'iyš ṣadiyq* "a righteous man," *tam-iym* "perfect" in his generation, and because he walked with God (Gen. 6:9; 7:1b)? Did Noah survive (live through) the flood by grace or by works?

The character of Noah is sketched briefly in Genesis 6:9. It reads like the sketch of the character of Job in Job 1:1. Indeed Noah, Job, and Danel became the *ma-šal* "parable" for the type of righteousness that makes God spare some people when he decides to mete out corporate punishment. It came to be said, as it reads in Ezekiel 14:14, 20, "Not even if those three righteous men—Noah, Job and Danel—were to come back from the grave. . . ."

The name *Noaḥ* indicates "rest." With an *m-* prefix of place, it gives *ma-no*ʷ*aḥ* "resting place." When, for instance, *Noaḥ* first sent out the dove from the ark to find out whether the flood had subsided from the surface of the earth, the dove could not find *ma-no*ʷ*aḥ* "a resting place" for her feet (Gen. 6:8–9). And so she returned to the ark. When the receding flood revealed the tops of the mountains, the ark itself found rest on Mount Ararat: *wat-ta-naḥ hat-tebah . . . 'al har-ey 'ararat* (Gen. 8:4).

The causative (*hi-f*ᵉ*'iyl* form) of the root (*nwḥ* » *he-niyaḥ*) occurs in Genesis 2:15: *way-yan-niḥ-e-hu*ʷ *b*ᵉ*-gan 'edɛn* "and he made him to rest in the garden of delight" (cf. Exod. 16:34). For Hebrew "made him to rest," the English version uses the verb "to place." It means "to put in a place and let it rest there." The reflex in Jukun is *na* "lie down"; in Yoruba it is *nà* in *na 'ra* "relax the body."

The name of *Noaḥ* has become a *mašal* for thrifty planning in an age of riotous living. The forward planning of *Noaḥ* is symbolized in the building of the *tebah* "ark." To take another example, the Civil Defense might build underground air-raid shelters—just in case. In fact, some householders in the United States designed air-raid shelters in the basements of their homes—just in case the Russians sent in missiles.

The imminent deluge has remained a permanent symbol of disaster looming ahead. Jesus used it to represent the coming of the day of judgment: "As it is in the days of Noah—they were eating and drinking, marrying and giving in marriage until the downpour[1] came—so will be the coming of the Son of Man" (Mt. 24:38).

To build a boat on dry land makes the boat-builder a target of ridicule. John Ricketts did that in Agbowa Ikosi.[2] Was he mad? He was a dreamer. But it is that boat on dry ground that will provide shelter in case of disaster, for tornadoes and overflowing streams do bring *may-im rabb-iym* "plentiful waters" to places normally considered far from the domain of water. "By faith Noah, being warned by God concerning events yet unseen, took heed and constructed an ark for the saving of his household; by this he condemned the world and became an heir of the righteousness which comes by faith" (Heb. 11:7).

If there is war in the town where you now live, in what ark will you find safety? It is not a theoretical question: it became a matter of life and death during the Nigerian civil war, during Idi Amin's invasion of the Kagera region of Tanzania, during the Tanzanian counterattack on Uganda. Where are you building an ark on dry ground that might become a shelter for your family in case you suddenly lost your well-paying job? Note that a *tebah* "box, chest" can be as big as a ship or as small as a money-box. King Josiah got such a money-box placed at the door of the Jerusalem temple so that worshipers might drop in contributions for the maintenance and repair of the temple. There may be no more floods to come, but disasters—natural and man-made—will always be with us. Are you building a *tebah* for that day?

The Greek-speaking translators of the Septuagint rendered both Hebrew *tebah* (Ijẹbu Yoruba *àtakpó* "stool": Aramaic *y*$^{e}$*tab* "sit") and *'aro*$^{w}$*n* "ark" (of the covenant) by the Greek word *kibot-os* "box," which was borrowed from Syriac *q*$^{e}$*but-a'*. Syriac *q*$^{e}$*but-a'* has reflexes in West Africa:

| | | |
|---|---|---|
| Hausa | *a-kwati* | "box" |
| Yoruba | *à-kpótí* | "box" |
| | *kpósí* | "coffin" |
| Igala | *ẹ-kpẹtẹ* | "stool" |
| Igbo | *o-kposi* | "ancestral stool" |

A box is certainly a place in which to keep things safe. That is the idea of the *tebah* Noah was instructed to build—a disaster relief fund, an emergency relief committee, the Red Cross, Christian Aid, Caritas. See what has happened in the drought-stricken Sahel, which has become a byword for disaster. Every family needs an ark; every community needs one or two people to concern themselves with it even in times of safety and security. Without *Noaḥ* we would have no *ma-no*$^{w}$*aḥ* when the fire comes next time.

## Mythology, Religion, and Science

The story of the marriages between the sons of the gods and the daughters of men begins at Genesis 6:1 and concludes at Genesis 6:7 or 6:8. Genesis 6:9 *'ellɛh to*$^{w}$*-l*$^{e}$*d-o*$^{w}$*t Noaḥ* "these are the generations of Noah" begins a different account. Whereas Genesis 6:1–7/8 suggests that Noah's survival was a result of Yahweh's *ḥen* "favor, grace" (: Yoruba *àánú* "mercy"), Genesis 6:9ff. attributes Noah's survival to his righteousness and his blamelessness: "Then Yahweh said to Noah: '. . . I have seen that you are righteous before me in this generation . . .' " (Gen. 7:1). Source critics studying this phenomenon say that there are two sources here, with clear evidence of theological editing. The redactor (editor) ended the story of the sons of God and the daughters of men by bringing in Noah: "But Noah found *ḥen* in the eyes of

Yahweh." But for that sentence it would have been impossible to explain why a wicked world did not come to an end.

We see here how mythology is pressed into the service of theology. When general disaster (floods, for instance) kills thousands—as still happens today—how do we account for the survival of those who are saved? *The Yahwist* states: Those who are blameless survive general disasters. *The Priestly Writers* state: Those who survive do so by the grace of God.

The interest of the underlying myth is neither moralism (as with the Yahwist) nor theology—God is merciful (as with the Priestly writers). The interest of myth is simply etiology. *Mythology* asks: "What is the cause of the alluvial forms noticeable in some land forms?" *Natural science* asks: "What killed the dinosaurs whose skeletons have been discovered in geological sites?"

Notice that the interest of the Yahwist and the Priestly writers includes human interest. The interest of mythology and science in nature results in amoral descriptions. When theology uses myth, therefore, it trims away the amoral details that do not serve its purpose. Take the natural phenomenon of the rainbow. *Mythology* asks: "Why is the rainbow so dazzling? And where does its arc begin? Where does it end?" *Physical science* asks: "What is the cause of the seven colors of the rainbow?" *Yahwist theology* asks: "Why did Yahweh put the rainbow in the sky?"[3]

Mythology, then, is the science and the theology of human beings in prescientific times. The age of science dawned when science and theology parted ways. When that happens, mythology dies.

Another example to consider is the Sabbath: Why do people not go to farm, to fish, or to hunt on certain days? *Mythology* says: "Because there are deadly spirits in the farm, in the river/sea, and in the forest on spirit-days. Anyone who goes to work on such days will die." *The Priestly Writers* say: "All work and no play makes Jack a dull boy. We need one day in seven for meetings and social gatherings, etc."

Religion legislates; science explains. Therefore the question: "Why do people not go to work on days of rest?" is actually a question of social sciences. The religious question is not "Why *do* people . . .?" but "Why *should* people not go to work on certain days?" To answer the question, religion (the Priest) uses myths. It is left to the theologian to clarify the meaning of the myths in order to show that the religious answer is not mere fancy but as serious and as valid as the answer of the social scientist.

When people wondered, "Why do snakes crawl on their bellies?" *mythology* answered: "Once upon a time. . . . And that is why snakes crawl on their bellies." *Religion* answered: "If the story does not concern human beings, I am not interested in the question." *Biological science* answered: "I am not interested in *why* snakes crawl on their bellies. I am curious to find out *how* they do it. I may be able to learn more about locomotion from it."

## The Covenant with Noah

What causes the rainbow, the *arc en ciel* as the French call it?

Before physics offered a scientific answer to that question, other types of answers had been offered. Since such questions are usually asked by inquisitive children, adults used the opportunity to give them ethical—not scientific—instruction. To the inquiry of children concerning the rainbow, then, the prescientific answer of the Hebrew parents was a theological answer: "God put the rainbow there."

What for? . . . Why? . . . Then follows the story of Noah and the flood and the decision of God at the end of the disaster:

> I will never again strike all living as I have done:
> As long as earth shall last
> Seed [time] and harvest
>    Cold [season] and heat [time]
> Summer and winter
>    Day and night
> Will never cease or rest [Gen. 8:21b–22].

As a sign of this promise, look at the rainbow: whenever you see it in the sky, threatening rain is held back for as long as the rainbow is visible. The observation that a heavy downpour and rainbow in the sky are mutually exclusive is accurate. The association of the *arc en ciel* with rain—imminent rain—is also accurate. Rainbows are most frequently seen when the dry season begins to win over from the rainy season. This characteristic of rainbows, which come out just when rain is being held in check, is what made the Jews use it as a symbol.

A symbol is a jumping-off point: from the observation of a natural phenomenon—the rainbow—to thoughts about the assurance of God that total destruction of all life by flood would never happen in the future as the geological configuration of the undulating earth suggests has happened before. It is actually this geological phenomenon that the story of the flood was told to explain. Nowadays a geography teacher would offer a geological explanation—earth formation and geological history. In times past a rabbi would tell the story of the flood—with a view to ethical instruction.

In these days of specialization, when a doctor no longer ministers as a priest and a priest no longer administers public health, scientists do not dabble in ethics or theology—not when they understand a question as demanding a scientific answer. Those who find the biblical explanations naïve are those who think that the ultimate questions in human life are questions of natural science. The biblical writers did not share this view: for them the ultimate questions were questions of human happiness. And to this they turned all inquiries.

Hence to the question, "Why were the blacks, who are said to have produced the first empire in human history, everywhere subject to the whites by the sixth century B.C.?" the biblical writers gave an answer with ethical/theological implications: Ham (the man from the hot climate), their ancestor, saw his father Noah naked and did not cover his nakedness. His brothers Shem and Yafet did. Ham's son was therefore cursed:

*’aru$^{w}$r k$^{e}$na‘an*
*‘ɛbɛd ‘$^{a}$bad-iym yi-h$^{e}$yɛh l$^{e}$-’Eḥ-ay-w*
*baru$^{w}$k YHWH ’$^{\varepsilon}$loh-ey šem*
*wiy-hiy k$^{e}$na‘an ‘ɛbɛd la-m-o$^{w}$.*

Accursed be Canaan.
A slave of slaves will he be to his brothers.
Blessed be Yahweh, the God of Shem,
And let Canaan be a slave to him [Gen. 9:25–26].*

*See also Appendix, section III, "The Sin of Ham and the Curse on Canaan."

Now that we human beings have seen how Egypt rose and fell, how Assyria rose and fell, how Babylon took over predominance from Assyria, its former overlords, how Persia defeated Babylon, and how the Greeks under Alexander swung the balance from Eastern-dominated imperialism to Western-dominated imperialism—Greece, Rome, Holy Roman empire, Portugal and Spain, Holland, England, and the seizure of the Americas, Africa, Asia, Australia and the Pacific by European conquistadores—we can now see that it is normal in the history of civilization and imperialism for the predominant civilization of today to yield to another tomorrow. The first in Jewish memory was the empire of Nimrod, the son of *Ku*$^{w}$*š*. Speaking as historians of civilization, we think it normal that the Semitic civilizations took over from the empire of Nimrod. The Jewish religious teachers looked for the ethical/theological factor: the imperialism of Nimrod was violent and its aspirations reached the point of hubris. And the gods do not like that!

Just as there are scientists who do not want ethics or theology brought to bear on any question, so there are historians who do not want ethics invoked as a cause of any historical event. For the question, "Why did the unified kingdom of Israel and Judah break up after the reign of Solomon?" they will accept sociological, political, economic, and military answers, but no ethical/religious answer suggesting that Solomon's marrying of foreign wives with foreign gods had anything to do with it. But ethics and theology was the supreme interest of the ancient Hebrews: in the medieval university theology was the queen of the sciences. Times have changed: physicists no longer write poetry and priests seldom teach theoretical physics. We have displaced as the ideal the person of many parts with the specialist who looks at every question from the point of view of his or her own specialist interest. Poetry is not now accepted as the mode of explaining science or reporting history. In fact, science has tried to free itself from expression through verbal symbols by adopting the abstract symbolization of Arabic numerals and subsequent additional nonverbal symbols.

*'aru*$^{w}$*r K*$^{e}$*na'an . . .*

Cursed be Canaan . . . [Gen. 9:25–26]

and

> *'od kol y^em-ey ha-'arεṣ . . .*
>
> All the remaining days of the earth . . . [Gen. 8:22]

are poetry. A modern poet might see things the same way. A modern scientist or historian would not. It is wrong to say that the biblical way of looking at things is old-fashioned. Modern poets and modern composers of songs still use the same frames of reference. Science has changed. Poetry and song do not change like that, for they exist on an ideological level, not dependent on the verifiability that is assisted by technological equipment.

## The Curse on Canaan

The story begins in Genesis 9:18: "The sons of Noah who came out of the ark were Shem, Ham and Japheth." It then puts the spotlight on Ham by saying: "Ham is the father [ancestor] of Canaan." The words of this spotlighting are significant: the passage does not read, "Ham is the father of Kush," nor "Ham is the father of *miṣ^er-ayim* [Egypt]," nor "Ham is the father of *pu^wt* [the Horn of Africa]"—any of which might have been appropriate, considering Genesis 10:6—but "Ham is the father of Canaan."

This prepares the reader's mind for what happened when Noah awoke from his sleep of wine and discovered what Ham had done (or not done) to him when he was naked. He said:

> Cursed be Canaan. . . .
> And may Canaan be his slave [Gen. 9:25, 27b].

Why curse Canaan when it was Ham who sinned? The truth is that the story is one of many told by the Hebrews to ridicule nations against whom they harbored a grudge. Four of the principal nations were: *(i) Egypt* (in the land of Ham)—The Hebrews hated the Egyptians because of what the Pharaoh who knew not Joseph did to their ancestors when they sojourned in Egypt. *(ii) Canaan*—The Hebrews despised the Canaanites. They considered them idolaters who could be annihilated in the name of Yahweh. *(iii) Moab*—The Hebrews abused the Moabites, saying that they were called *Moab* (cf. *me-'ab*, "from father") because they were born from an incestuous relationship between Lot and his two daughters (Gen. 19:30–38). For what the Moabites did to the children of Israel on their way from Egypt, see Numbers 22. (To say that *me-'ab* is the etymology of *Moab* is an example of folk etymology.)[4] *(iv) Babɛl*—The Hebrews saw in the ruins of the ziggurats of Babylon a point of departure for suggesting that Babylon fell because it was aspiring to the power of heaven. Hence the story of the tower of Babel, which involved also folk etymology on the name *Babɛl*. It was forced; for *balal* "he confused" does not explain the name of *Babɛl*.

## Children of Adam and Sons of Noah

The Yoruba call a well-behaved, cultured person *Ọmọlúwàbí*. The traditional analysis of the term as *ọmọ (ti) Noaḥ bí* "the children born by Noah" is corroborated by linguistic analysis: If Hebrew *N-m-r-d (Nimrod)* = Yoruba *L-m-r-d (Lámúrúdu),* then Hebrew *N-w-ḥ (Noaḥ) = L-w (-lúwà)* in Yoruba *ọmọ-lúwà-bí* "child born by Noah." The *-úwà* in *ọmọlúwàbí* is not Yoruba *ùwà* "character"; and *-bí* is not Yoruba *bí* "like, as," neither of which helps to make sense of *ọmọlúwàbí*.

We are not now thinking of the sons of Noah as ancestors of the blacks, the Middle East Asiatics, and the Europeans. The liberal Jewish concept of *Noaḥ-i-des* "sons of Noah" provides a contrast with the term "sons of Adam" (or "children of Abraham"). The sons of Adam were so evil that God destroyed them in the flood. Those who were saved—the sons of Noah—were, therefore, sons of the good man. These are the ones the Yoruba call *ọmọ-lúwà-bí*—well-behaved persons.[5]

It is not religion that makes one a *Noaḥ-id*, an *ọmọlúwàbí*: it is not that Jews are *ọmọlúwàbí*, or that Gentiles are *ọmọ Ádámọ̀* "crafty evil human beings." Jews and Gentiles are included in both "children of Adam" and "sons of Noah." The distinctive Hebrew/Jewish category is "children of Abraham." The distinctive Christian category is not "son of Abraham" (Jew) but "believer in Jesus as Lord and Savior." The distinctive Islamic category is that of those who reject all divine lords except one God and acknowledge Muhammad as his apostle. A Christian must therefore be willing to recognize an *ọmọlúwàbí* upon meeting one. The *ọmọlúwàbí*'s character will be found acceptable no matter what the person's religion is.

How important is the distinction of faith? What does Christ want us to be—Christians or *ọmọlúwàbí?* How does one become an *ọmọlúwàbí*—by upbringing, by conversion to Christianity, or how? Is a Christian automatically an *ọmọlúwàbí?* To make the question no longer theoretical: Do you consider the Boers of the Dutch Reformed Church in South Africa *ọmọlúwàbí?* Do you consider them to be Christian?

Do you know some unbelievers who are *ọmọlúwàbí?* Between such people—the *ọmọlúwàbí*—and others in whom the influence of the first Adam is strong, the *ọmọ Ádámọ*, on which group would you spend more effort trying to make converts to Christianity? What are the reasons for your choice?

# 7

# The Sons of *'Ebɛr* and the Sons of *Qayin*

*'Ebɛr* is the name of the ancestor of the *b*$^{e}$*n-ey 'Ebɛr* "sons of Eber." These were, in the Bible, the *'ib*$^{e}$*r-iym* "the Hebrews" (Gen. 10:21, 24; 11:14–17). *'Ebɛr,* the name of their ancestor, is comparable to the various names by which the wandering Fulani of West Africa are known: *Abore* in Nigeria (Bornu) and in Chad; *Bororo* in Nigeria (Adamawa); *Fula* in Senegal and the Gambia; *Peul* in Guinea; *Pulo* in Senegal and the Gambia (plural *Ful-be).* This last is what they call themselves. Their language is called *Ful-ful-de* in Nigeria.

The *'-b-r* root in the name *'Ebɛr* and in the name *'ib*$^{e}$*r-iy* "Hebrew" occurs in

| | | |
|---|---|---|
| Hebrew | *'abar* | "cross over, trespass, pass on, pass by" |
| | *'abo*$^{w}$*r su*$^{w}$*fah* | "wind whistling by"[1] |
| Twi | *borọ* | "to trespass" |
| | *borọ-fo* | "passer by, alien, European" |
| Bachama | *puro* | "to exceed" |
| Yoruba | *ạfárá* | "bridge" |
| | *Ìbarà* | "ford" |
| | *ìbàrà-(mú)* | "across (the nose)" |
| | *ẹ̀bùrú* | "short cut" (across an area) |
| | *afẹ́rẹ́*[2] | "breeze" |

The *'ib*$^{e}$*r-iym* got that name because, being nomads, they were always passing by the cities of the Canaanites and never settling among them. *'-b-r* means "pass on, pass by" in Judges 19:12b, 18a, and in Ruth 4:1. The man of Levi who was going with his *piylɛgɛš* "concubine" (Yoruba *kpáńṣágà* "adultery") from Bethlehem in Judah to the hill country of Ephraim refused the suggestion of his servant that they should turn aside in *Y$^{e}$bu$^{w}$s* and seek lodging for a night, since the sun was already going down:

> We shall not turn aside into a city of strangers
> who are not part of *b$^{e}$n-ey yiṣera'el.* No.
> We will *'aBar* until *Gib$^{e}$'ah* [Judg. 19:12b].
>
> *way-ya-'aB$^{e}$r-u$^{w}$ way-ye-lek-u$^{w}$*
> *wat-ta-bo' la-hɛm haš-šɛmɛš 'eṣɛl hag-gib$^{e}$'ah 'ašɛr*
> *le-binyamin way-ya-sur-u$^{w}$ šam. . . .*
>
> And they passed on and walked on.
> And the sun set upon them near Gibeah
> of Benjamin, where they turned in [for lodgings] . . .
> [vs. 14].

In the square of Gibe'ah where they settled, he explained to the old man who accosted him: " *'oB$^{e}$r-iym* are we from Bethlehem of Judah to the hill country of Ephraim. That is where I am from" (vs. 18). The *'ib$^{e}$r-iym* were *'oB$^{e}$r-iym* "passers by": *'oB$^{e}$r-ey dɛrɛk* "those who pass by" (Lam. 1:12a).

Thus Abram on his way from Haran "passed through" the land to the place at Shechem: *"way-ya-'abor 'Abram* through the land to the place at Shechem, to the oak of Moreh. At that time the Canaanites were in the land" (Gen. 12:6). When he broke camp from the oak of Moreh he went toward the hill country but skirted the cities: "*way-yeṭ 'ahol-o$^{w}$* with Bethel to the west and Ai to the east" (Gen. 12:8). He bypassed both Bethel and Ai, like a true *'ib$^{e}$r-iy.*

What the *'ib$^{e}$r-iym* were in the land of *Ḥam* (Egypt and Canaan), the *Abore/Bororo* have been in the land of *Ḥam* all over the West African *savannah* (= Hebrew *š$^{e}$felah*)—the country of the Soninke, the Mandingo, and the Hausa. Their route over four millennia skirted the Sahara (see map on p. 65). The *Bororo* are not "men of the desert," *bedouin* who raise camels.[3] The *bedouin* of the Sahara are the Tuareg, not the *Bororo.* "The

Suggested Route from the Ultimate Source
of Fulani Migrations to West Africa

patriarchs kept sheep and goats and were beginning to lead a settled life.''[4]

The debate as to whether the *Abore* (the nomadic Fulani) are Sudanic natives or ''Hamitic'' immigrants into the Sudan (the ''Hamitic hypothesis'' in African history) or whether Fulfulde is a Hamitic or a West Atlantic (Sudanic) language can be illuminated by remembering what Isaiah the Israelite prophet called the Hebrew language. He refers to Hebrew as *ś$^{e}$fat k$^{e}$na‘an* ''the speech of Canaan'' (Isa. 19:18), because the *‘ib$^{e}$r-iym* adopted *ś$^{e}$fat k$^{e}$na‘an* when they invaded Canaan.

Is it not possible that the *Abore* adopted the language of West Sudan when their wanderings took them to those parts? Did the adoption of the language of Canaan make the Hebrews Canaanites culturally? (To some extent it did—with prophets and Rechabites as voices in the wilderness.) Does the adoption of a West Atlantic form of speech make the *Abore/Bororo* Sudanic blacks culturally? For the Ful-be *siire,* the *Pula/Pulo/Fulani* who settled down, the answer is Yes. (Fulfulde *siire* is cognate with Yoruba *silẹ̀,* Hebrew *šalu$^{w}$y* ''settled,'' like wine on the lees.) However, the *Abore/Bororo* who did not settle down but continued as *‘oB$^{e}$r-iym* can be regarded as culturally Sudanic blacks to only a slight degree.

The distinctiveness of the *Bororo* way of life in spite of millennia of contact with farming communities of West Africa must be remarked upon. They are milk-drinking West Africans. They are seldom cited in books on African traditional religion. The classification of Fulfulde as a Niger-Congo rather than ''Hamitic'' language does not nullify the significance of this distinctiveness, for, in the words of W. F. Albright, ''Race, culture, and language are heterogeneous entities.''[5]

The southern limit of the Hamito-Semitic languages is not the Niger-Benue confluence but the Atlantic Guinea Coast. The *Abore/Bororo* are successors (descendants) of the *b$^{e}$n-ey ‘EBɛr:* the Pula are the relics of the *‘Apiru.* They have been traversing Hamito-Semitic terrain since Abrahamic times. ''Language may be used with caution to prove an original physical association between different groups of men,'' Albright says. ''Of course, it is no longer necessary to emphasize the fact that a common linguistic inheritance does not necessarily carry with it a common racial origin, since language may be borrowed whereas physical inheritance cannot."[6] The physical features of the Fulani are atypical in West Africa.

The *'Apiru (Habiru, Hapiru)* were found everywhere in the Ancient Near East: in upper and lower Mesopotamia, in Syria, in Palestine, in Egypt. The word *'Apiru* is to *Pulo* (singular) phonologically as Hebrew *'apar* (Akkadian *eperu*) "dust" is to Acholi *apulu* "dust" (Yoruba *erùkpẹ̀* "dust"). For the plural *Ful-be,* compare the plural of *'Apiru* in Ugaritic: *'prm.*[7] The pluralizing suffix *-be* in the Fulfulde language is equivalent to the *-m* in *'prm.*

## *Hɛbɛl*

In Genesis *HɛBɛl* was a *ro'ɛh ṣo'n* "a feeder of sheep and goats" (Gen. 4:2). *YaBal* was the ancestor of those who dwell in *'ohɛl* "tents" and own *mi-qᵉnɛh* "cattle" (Gen. 4:20).

As *Yuʷbal* is the ancestor of all who play the *kinnoʷr* "lyre" and the *'uʷgab* "pipe," we know that his name is formed from the same consonantal root as Hebrew *yoʷbɛl* "ram's horn" (: Grebo *ble* "cow"; Gã *blɛ* "horn"; Twi *abɛn* "horn"; Si-swati *i-m-pala-m-pala* "horn trumpet"; Owerri Igbo *ebulu* "ram"; Onitsha Igbo *ebunu* "ram"; Fulfulde *m-bala* "sheep"; Serer *mbal* "sheep" and also the name of the small antelope called *impala* in the Bantu area).

*YaBal,* the name of the first tent-dwelling cowherd, is a variation of the same root as *Yuʷbal* and *yoʷbɛl.* Hebrew *nebɛl* "flute" is another variant *(Y-Bl, n-Bl),* and *Hɛbɛl* is still another *(Y-Bl, n-Bl, h-Bl).* We expect these triconsonantal roots to appear as biconsonantal bases in West Africa. Hence:

*Hɛbɛl—Pulo, Ful-be* (the pluralizing suffix *-be: -wa* in Hausa: prefix *ba-* in *Ba-ntu)*
*'Ebɛr—A-bore*

We can cross-check. *Hɛbɛl* brought for sacrifice some of the *bᵉkor-oʷt* "firstborn" (Igbo *Ọkpara* "firstborn") of his *ṣo'n* (Gã *tsina* "cattle"; Yoruba *ẹran ọ̀-sìn* "domestic animals") and some of their *ḥelɛb* "cream, milk, fatty portion" (: Zulu *hlope* "white, fair"; Yoruba *èlùbọ́* "yam flour"). The phrase *pᵉriy 'adam-ah* “fruit of the soil,” from which *Qayin* brought *mi-n$^{e}$ḥah* “gift offering” (: Efik *ẹnọ* “gift”), shows Owerri Igbo *m-kpuru* “fruit” for Hebrew *p$^{e}$riy* “fruit.” We mention these in order to show that we are not expounding *Qayin:Ò-gún/Hεbεl:Pulo* in isolation. The mythology is Hamito-Semitic. And the myth-makers offer etymologies (albeit folk etymologies) to validate their myths. The connection between *Hεbεl, yabal,* and *‘Ebεr* is that shepherds and cattle nomads tend to be *‘oB$^{e}$r-iym*. So were the *‘ib$^{e}$r-iym*. So have been the *Abore* and the *Bororo*.

The conventional interpretation of the name of *Hεbεl* is from Hebrew *hεbεl* “breath,” the same word that recurs in Ecclesiastes: *hεbεl/hεBεl haBal-iym* “vanity/vanity of vanities.” How does *hεBεl* “breath” fit into the story of *Hεbεl* in Genesis 4? In Ecclesiastes *hεbεl* means “fleeting breath, passing breath, vanishing breath.” It passes; it does not endure. It passes and leaves no residue. Hence:

> *hak-kol hεbεl u$^{w}$-r$^{e}$‘-u$^{w}$t ru$^{w}$aḥ*
> *w$^{e}$-’eyn yit$^{e}$r-o$^{w}$n taḥat haš-šamεš.*
>
> Everything is as fleeting as breath. It is like trying to eat wind: there is nothing left when the balance sheet is drawn. So is everything under the sun [Eccles. 2:11b].

The words *hεbεl* and *r$^{e}$‘-u$^{w}$t ru$^{w}$aḥ* doubly picture passing breath and the futility of eating wind, for *r$^{e}$‘-u$^{w}$t* comes from the same root, *r‘h* “to eat” (of animals: Igbo *-ri* “eat” of men) as *ro‘-o$^{w}$t* in Job 1:14b: *ha-’aton-o$^{w}$t ro‘-o$^{w}$t ‘al y$^{e}$d-ey-hεm* “the donkeys grazing at their side.” After *hεbεl* and *ru$^{w}$aḥ,* there is no *yiter-o$^{w}$n* “nothing left over,” no excess of income over expenditure. “Wodaabe are described by their sedentary neighbours as the wind which blows through the bush; when they are gone, all that remains is a few stripped branches and a patch of bare earth.”[8] This is Hebrew *hεbεl* “breath”; this is Hebrew *‘abo$^{w}$r su$^{w}$fah* “a passing wind.” Hebrew *‘br* is used in Habakkuk 1:11a:

> *’az ḥalaf ka-ru$^{w}$aḥ way-ya-$^{‘a}$Bor.*
>
> Then they sweep by like the wind and go on (R.S.V.).
> Then they pass on like the wind and are gone (N.E.B.).

*Hɛbɛl* is "vanity" because *hɛbɛl* is "vanishing breath"—insubstantial, impermanent, nonlasting. Wealth is *hɛbɛl.* Fame is *hɛbɛl.* Knowledge is *hɛbɛl.* Pleasure is *hɛbɛl.* As *Qayin* is the *heros eponymous* of all farmers who cultivate the soil and build *'iyr* (:Yoruba *ìlú* "city"), so is *Hɛbɛl* the *heros eponymous* of all nomads who, like *'aboʷr suʷfah,* are here today and gone tomorrow.

> The pastoral Bodaado has no sense of attachment to a specific plot of land he calls his home. Rather, he is at home in any of the favourite pastures where he or his father have tended their herds, in any of the markets where his women folk sell milk, and on the cattle tracks *(burti,* sing. *burtol)* and foot paths *(laabi,* sing. *laawel)* which join them.[9]

*Tuʷbal Qayin* is to *Qayin* as *Yabal* and *Yuʷbal* are to *Hɛbɛl.* As *Hɛbɛl* left no children, *Yabal* and *Yuʷbal* are credited to the line of *Qayin,* the same line as *Tuʷbal Qayin.*

We may raise the question, "Where did *Qayin* find a wife when there were on earth only himself and his parents?" The answer is that the story is not dealing with the story of a single nuclear family. *'Adam, Ḥawwah, Qayin,* and *Hɛbɛl* are not personal names of any individuals who ever lived. *'Adam* represents all male human beings in their strength; *Ḥawwah* represents all birth-giving female human beings; *Qayin* stands for all settled farming peoples using iron implements; *Hɛbɛl* stands for all nomadic shepherds. After all, in Swahili *Fulani* (cf. *Fula, Pulo, Ful-be*) merely means "someone, so and so."

## *Qayin* and *Hɛbɛl*

The godly life is nomadic life.

The *bᵉn-ey 'eBɛr* "Hebrews" (sons of *'eBɛr)* were seminomadic herdsmen; the Canaanites were *(i)* farmers inland, and *(ii)* importers and exporters on the coast. Hence *hak-kᵉna'an-iy* "the Canaanite" occurs in Hebrew idiom with the meaning "(overseas) merchant" in Proverbs 31:24. Their race produced the Phoenician and Carthaginian sea merchants and—in modern life—the Lebanese traders (e.g., those of Lebanon Street, Ibadan, Nigeria).

Cattle nomads and settled farmers were frequently unfriendly in antiquity. The cattle nomads respected no boundaries but trampled along wherever the grass was greener. They were on a perennial pilgrimage: their doctrine, voiced by Moses, that everywhere was holy ground conflicted with the doctrine of the settled farmers (see, e.g., the Egyptians, who invented surveying) that you must respect my own grounds (land, country) as holy to me while I respect your own grounds (land, country) as holy to you. Everywhere the nomads roamed with their sheep and goats, donkeys and cattle, the settled farmer hated what their invasion did to his farms. It is such a situation that made the Yoruba say:

> *Ọmọ, onílè tẹ̀ ẹ́ jẹ́ jẹ́;*
> *Àjèjì tẹ̀ ẹ́ gìdìgìdì.*
>
> The child of the landowner steps on it softly, softly;
> The alien tramples on it *gìdìgìdì* [roughshod].

Take the Ful-be, who are found in Senegal, Guinea, the Gambia, northern Sierra Leone, northern Liberia, northern Ivory Coast, Mauritania, northern Ghana, Niger, northern Nigeria, Cameroon, and Chad. Where is their home? To what *omenala* "customs" (= what is done in the land) are they committed? What *nsọ ala* "taboo" (= what is sacred to the land) do they respect? A race within a race in every country of West Africa—straight nose among the flat-nosed, nose rings among people who wear only earrings, milk drinkers among those who are not. They do not stop long enough to belong. They do not even want to belong in the cities or the towns or the village councils. They are the eternal passersby. This is the meaning of *'-b-r ('eBɛr: Abore, Bororo),* the name of the first Hebrew.

The nomads clashed now and then with the settled villagers and townspeople. The history of the medieval empires of West Africa shows that they defeated the settled villagers by burning their thatched huts at night. They thus built the empires of Ghana, Mali, and Songhai. These events, however, took place after the domestication of the horse, and the use of cavalry by savannah land-raiders tipped the scales of warfare in favor of the savannah nomads.

Before the horse became available for cavalry charges, the farmers were, apparently, victorious over the nomads. That is what Jewish memory states in the story of *Qayin* and *Hεbεl.* To say that *Qayin* was the elder brother is a way of saying that he was the stronger. And *Qayin* was a farmer. *Hεbεl* was a shepherd. We know this from the products each brought to sacrifice to God.

We are not told that *Qayin* brought poor farm products to sacrifice to God while *Hεbεl* brought fat sheep to sacrifice. Why, then, did God accept the sacrifice of the shepherd but not the sacrifice of the farmer? There is no hint of any moral or theological reason. But there is a culture-history reason. As this story is being told by the descendants of *'eBεr,* the eternal cattle nomad, all they are saying is that to them nomadic life is preferable to settled life. The way the story of *Qayin* and *Hεbεl* is told, with the curse attributed to the farmer, practically affirms that settled life in villages and cities was a godforsaken life, an accursed life, a life of slavery to the soil. The best life is the life of the nomadic herdsman.

Christianity inherited this view from the Hebrews through the Jews. To be in the world but not of it is to live like a Bororo among the Hausa or among the Bachama. Farmers do not live like that; farmers are in the world and are of it. The *'ib$^{e}$r-iy* is naturally a citizen of two countries (ancestral home and present place on the savannah pilgrimage); the farmer is naturally a citizen of only one country (as symbolized by the fact that the ancestor is buried below the sleeping room). Seeing the farmer at work on his farm, the *'ib$^{e}$r-iym* postulated that the farmer was serving some punishment. Who, they wonder, would be a farmer unless the person who, because of some misdeed, has been expelled from the garden of bliss *la-'abod '$^{ε}$t ha-'adamah* "to work as a slave on the soil" (Gen. 3:23)?

You do not need to preach to the Bororo that they must live a life of pilgrimage. They naturally live such a life. J. E. G. Sutton comments that rather than being "the fabled founders of empires and the presumed authors of technological feats [according to the Hamitic hypothesis], some of the present-day pastoral tribes in eastern Africa [are] peoples with very frugal material cultures and uncentralized political systems."[10] One cause of conflict between Christian ideals and the reality of the lives of Christians is that in most parts of the world those who declare themselves Christians are by and large those who love the settled life. In missionary times this could not be so. All missionaries have left home and homeland. When they preach to settled farmers about the need to set out on a pilgrimage of life, the message encounters deepseated cultural barriers. The only pilgrimages that settled farmers participate in are religious festivals, as is suggested in the following terminology:

| | | |
|---|---|---|
| Arabic | *ḥaj* | "pilgrimage" |
| Hebrew | *ḥag* | "pilgrim feast, pilgrimage festival" (plural *hagg-iym*) |
| Egyptian | *w3g* | "religious festival" |
| Freetown Creole | *à-wùjọ* | "family cook" (Yoruba *àwùjọ,* "assembly") |
| Bini | *ugie* | "festival" |

Preaching a life of Christian pilgrimage to the agricultural tribes of Africa is like preaching a life of nomadic herdsmen to Pharaonic Egyptians: "To sit down to a meal with *ʻib*$^{e}$*r-iym* was *to*$^{w}$*-ʻeb-ah* ["abomination"] to Egyptians. Every herdsman is an abomination to the Egyptians" (Gen. 43:32). The agricultural tribes of Africa are Egyptians at heart. The *ʻib*$^{e}$*r-iym* of Africa are the Fulani in West Africa, the Masai in East Africa, the Galla and Somali in the Horn, and the Nguni people in the south. It is evident that the settler Christians do not know how to preach a life of pilgrimage to these natural pilgrims.

How did Christianity lose this natural connection with a life of pilgrimage? When did it become impossible to recruit disciples who would go out carrying only their staves—no purse, no luggage—as Islam was spread in West Africa by the West African *ʻib*$^{e}$*r-iym?* Canaan is strong among the farming peoples of Africa, who listen to the gospel that sets one free but tame it to sedentary ways before they live it.

To trace the change one must go back to Lot's choice of city life in Sodom, and then forward to the time when the children of Israel, once in the promised land, tired of being themselves—nomads without kings and without fixed temples—and actively yearned to be like other nations, settled within permanent territorial borders and ruled by a powerful king as Egypt had been.

When John Wesley observed that the Anglican priesthood in England was full of settlers, he devised in the Wesleyan church the circuit system to ensure that no Wesleyan clergyman became an agricultural Canaanite. The Wesleyan circuit system required every Wesleyan minister to be moved from his station after a stay of no more than five years. If he stayed longer in one station, he would soon become a *Fulani n gida* "a town Fulani," settled and sedentary.

Do you know any other way of recruiting disciples? Can you go among a farmer people and call, "Follow me," and find that straightaway they would leave their hoes and follow you? Will a man who has just planted yams do that? Can you get farmers to set out with only staff and no purse? The Fulani people traveled on foot from Senegal to Cameroon. And some are still walking from Sokoto to Ibadan in Nigeria. They are not afraid to camp where night finds them or to beg where their supply finishes. The Sahel drought has brought to Guinea coast cities light-skinned Africans who beg not apologetically but confidently. Didn't Jesus say to the seventy that in whatever town they found themselves they should ask for hospitality, thereby discovering if there were in the place any sons of *'islaam?* Is there today a preacher of the gospel doing just that?

What the story of *Qayin* murdering *Hεbεl* tries to say is that a decision not to move on but to stay put in life makes one a murderer of idealists on a pilgrimage. To offer an example: when a head of state sits tight instead of resigning or relinquishing office, he invariably becomes a tyrant. He imprisons prophets and kills the poor.

Note that the Boers in South Africa decided to be settlers—and the British in Rhodesia. Mau Mau was organized against white settlers in Kenya. In West Africa, on the contrary, whites were banned from acquiring freehold land. They were allowed only leasehold land. If today the blacks in Nigeria are independent, and the blacks in South Africa are suffering, it is because white settlers *(Qayin)* arrived in the Cape in 1652 to compete with Zulu cattle people. *Qayin* still kills *Hεbεl.* The Zulu are a part of the *N-guni* people, and the Zulu word *N-guni* is cognate with Hebrew *mi-qᵉnεh* "cattle."

What does the contrast between the sacrifice of *Qayin* and the sacrifice of *Hεbεl* suggest to us? What sacrifice are we preparing for God—farm products or pastoral products, fruits of slavery or fruits of freedom? Genesis seldom preaches directly, but makes its point indirectly by parables and myths. It curses all settlers, all who are afflicted by what Ọbafemi Awolọwọ of the Unity Party of Nigeria once called the tenacity of office, all who prefer the regularity of the waters of the Nile to the uncertainty of *Ḥorɛb* with its commandments.

Unfortunately *Hɛbɛl,* whose sacrifice was accepted by God, had no son. He was murdered by the settler farmer before he could "settle in life." The cattle nomad tradition has an unsure future: idealistic movements come and go while bureaucratic systems gather moss. Modern governments are trying to check the nomadism of nomads: we say that cattle ranching is better than nomadic pastoralism. And how can nomadic herdsmen survive with the modern system of political boundaries, passports, visas, entry permits, and so on? *Qayin* is still killing *Hɛbɛl.*

You need a staff to be a shepherd but you need *ọkọ́* "hoe" and *àdá* "machete" to do *iṣẹ́ àgbẹ̀* "farm work." The smith produced agricultural equipment. The Yoruba therefore say that Ògún is

*aládǎ méjì.*
*Ó ń fi ọ̀kan ṣán oko;*
*Ó ń fi ọ̀kan yẹ 'nà.*

The owner of two machetes.
With one he clears the bush,
With the other he weeds the path.

## *Tuʷbal Qayin*

As we have seen earlier, there are two *Qayin*s in Genesis: *Qayin*, the farmer, and *Tuʷbal Qayin,* the blacksmith: "He was the ancestor of all those who hammer all gold and bronze and iron into implements" (Gen. 4:22).

The farmer came before the blacksmith because, in fact, farming was practiced before the iron age. Before the iron age, farmers used wooden hoes, wooden plows, and stone knives and axes. When Tubal Cain (Hahm *Kuno)* discovered how to smelt iron, a technological revolution in farming took place: iron hoes and cutlasses displaced wooden hoes and stone-tipped axes.

When, therefore, Yoruba farmers prepared for farming, they presented their iron hoes and cutlasses at the shrine of *Ògún,* the ancestor of all who hammer iron into farming implements. It was in Canaan (and Egypt) that such a god was worshiped. Real *'ib^er-iym* had no need of his aid. A wooden staff sufficed to ward off a lion from the herd. When the farmer with iron knife and ax confronted the shepherd with wooden staff, however, the farmer killed the shepherd.

A profound reason for Christian preaching against the veneration of *Ògún,* therefore, is that *Ògún* is *Qayin,* and those who worship him with heart and soul will kill people on life-assignments that require carrying nothing but a staff. The Hahm people in the area of Nok called *Kuno* "Satan." The Hebrews said that *Qayin* was driven from the presence of Yahweh.

The Ebira *Egene* was a class of despised smiths who did work in iron over a wide area of Igbirra country.[11] It was not only the sons of *'Ebɛr* who wandered over a vast area of Africa; the sons of *Qayin* did the same. And the Hebrews told us that they wandered far when they said that Yahweh cursed *Qayin* in these words: "A fugitive and a wanderer shall thou be on the earth" (Gen. 4:12b). The Genesis narrative disposed of *Qayin* very briefly: "And *Qayin* went out from the presence of Yahweh and dwelt in the land of Nod, east of *'Edɛn.*"

Since *Qayin* went out of the presence of Yahweh, and the Hebrews did not, the Hebrews knew no more of the fortunes or misfortunes of *Qayin* and his descendants in Africa. After Genesis 4:17–24, the Hebrew writers closed the book on the history of metallurgy, urbanization, agriculture, and animal husbandry in Africa and went back to *'adam* and *Ḥawwah* (Gen. 4:25) to pick up their own story, which was ideologically anticivilization, antitechnology, and antiplastic art. Try as they would, however, they could not help but keep running into the heritage of *Qayin:*

> It has long been known that Cain cannot be separated from the tribe of the Kenites often mentioned in the Old Testament. Cain is the embodiment of the ancestor of the Kenites, and therefore it is scarcely thinkable that the Yahwist, in whose time the Kenites still existed, was not also thinking, in his story about Cain, of this tribe and its curious fate. . . .

> The Kenites were a difficult riddle to the Israelites. They, too, like the Israelites, were worshippers of Yahweh, perhaps even before Israel. Their relatives, the Rechabites (II Kings 10:15ff.; Jer., ch. 35; I Chron. 2:55), were even especially fanatic zealots of Yahweh. . . . Coming themselves from the south they had indeed joined the desert wandering of the Israelites (Num. 10:29ff.), but they never really achieved a sedentary life.[12]

Their wandering in the Arabian desert was noted by the Israelites, who were ignorant of their wandering in Africa. The Hahm of the area of Nok recognized *Tubal Qayin*'s handiwork in the furnaces of *Kuno. Tubal Qayin* flourished as *Ògún* among the Yoruba, where he is revered as an *òrìṣà* of ironworkers, and *Akin* "valiant man" (:Middle Egyptian *qny* "elite corps"). If in Yoruba mythology the home of *Ògún* is in Ire in Ekiti, the center of occurrence of *Akin* personal names is Ondo.[13] And there I would locate the land that in Genesis is called—by the usual folk etymology of Genesis—the land of Nod (see map on p. 77). We are told in Genesis that the land of Nod is east of *'Edɛn*. This says nothing, really; for where is *'Edɛn* itself?

Cattle pastoralism originated in Africa during the Neolithic subpluvial era, ca. 7000 B.C.–3000 B.C. There was agriculture and cattle pastoralism in the Sahara "before Egypt ever embarked on her course toward village life."[14]

> In the newly-greened Sahara between about 7000 and 3000 B.C. . . . there were two adaptive economic strategies pursued in varying degrees by Saharan peoples . . . —cultivation of barley and dates, and grazing of sheep, goats and cattle. In the central and northern Sudan where rainfall was greater than in Upper Egypt, a relatively continuous blanket of savanna vegetation . . . stretched from the Nile west into the heart of the desert, to Uweinat, Gilf Kebir, Tibetsi and Haggar. In such country the free-ranging cattle pastoralism still typical of the Sudan and eastern Africa flourished and cattle were doubtless always relatively more important than agricultural cultigens like barley. Such is the case among the modern Nuer and Dinka.[15]

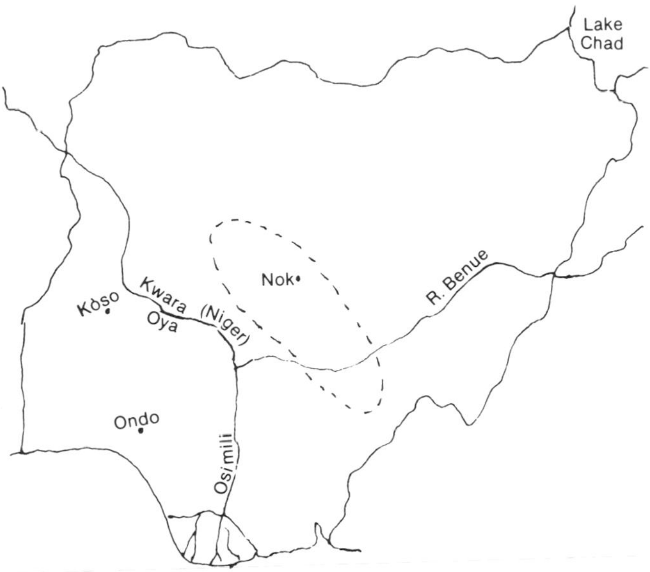


Nigeria Showing Nok,
Ondo, and Ọyọ Ile (*Kòso*)

We must note that in carrying us straight from Ádam *(ri's-oʷn 'adam : Àdàmú òrìṣà)* to *Qayin (Ògún)* the farmer and *Hɛbɛl (Fula)* the shepherd, the Genesis primeval history has jumped over a million years of prehistory from *Zinjanthropus* through the Paleolithic and has landed us straight in a Neolithic setting:

*Ògún* was a tiller of a *dom,*
*Pulo* was a shepherd of sheep.

The Hebrew writers quickly disposed of both of them by making *Qayin* kill *Hɛbɛl* and sending *Qayin* off into exile in the land of Nod. This is a dramatist's way of removing some of the characters permanently from the stage. The stage was being cleared for Hebrew history, not world history. *Ògún* and *Pulo* continued their own history in Africa: *Pulo* skirted the Sahara via the Maghreb to the Sahel; *Ògún* traversed the Sahel from Kush to Nok to Koso and Ondo (see map on p. 77).

Copper tools are known in Upper Egypt from about 5500 B.C. Around 3500 B.C. true smelted and cast copper tools appeared for the first time in Egypt. "Like agriculture 2000 years before, metallurgy had developed first in other regions like the Mediterranean and Iranian Plateau, and spread into Egypt via trade with foreign lands."[16] Joseph got to Egypt (sometime between 1720 and 1550 B.C.) because there were Ishmaelite traders from Gilead in northeast Jordan passing through Palestine on their way to Egypt. And there was a route "across the Sinai between the Nile Valley and Southern Palestine."[17] Maadi in Egypt developed a copper industry between 3600 and 3000 B.C. because of contact with the copper mines of Sinai, for it was located along the principal route to the Sinai mines.

The descendants of *Qayin* are therefore still flourishing in the land of Nod: witness the *Egene,* the caste of despised smiths who do iron working over a wide area of Igbirra country in Nigeria.[18] The annual festival of *Ògún* can still be witnessed in Ondo any September. And if the *'ibᵉr-iym* stopped being wandering Aramaeans long ago, the sons of *'Ebɛr* in Africa are still moving on with their cattle from Fouta Jallon *(beyt 'ayyal-oʷn)* and Fouta Toro in Senegal through every country of West Africa.

# 8

# *Balala-balala*: The *Babεl* of Tongues

How can all the earth be *safah 'εḥat* "one speech" (Gen. 11:1a) when we are given in Genesis 10 a list of the following:

| | |
|---|---|
| *b$^{e}$n-ey Yafεt* | "the sons of Yafet" (10:5) |
| *b$^{e}$n-ey Ḥam* | "the sons of Ham" (10:20) |
| *b$^{e}$n-ey Šem* | "the sons of Shem" (10:32) |
| *li-mi-š$^{e}$paḥ-ot-am* | "clan by clan" (cf. Se-tswana *tshaba* "tribe") |
| *li-l$^{e}$šon-ot-am* | "according to their tongues" (i.e., language by language) (Arabic *lis-aan*, Middle Egyptians *nas*, Ngas *lis* "tongue") |
| *b$^{e}$-'ar$^{e}$ṣ-ot-am* | "territory by territory" |
| *l$^{e}$-go$^{w}$-ey-hεm* | "according to their political groupings" (Ngas *go*; Mwaghavul *gu* "person") |

The internal evidence suggests that Genesis 11:1–9 was not originally a sequel to Genesis 10, but an independent story whose purpose was:

*i.* to provide a diatribe against *Babεl* "Babylon," the oppressor of *Y$^{e}$hu$^{w}$dah* "Judah" from 596 B.C. to 536 B.C. Similar side-blows against *Babεl* can be seen in (*a*) Isaiah's symbolic picture of *heylel bɛn šaḥar* "the shiner, son of Dawn" (Isa. 14:3–16) whose fall from eminence he saw, and (*b*) the story of Nebuchadnessar falling from grace to grass. See Revelation 14:8, where John heard an angel say: "Fallen, fallen is *Babɛl* the great, which made all the nations drink from the wine of the wrath of her harlotry." *Babɛl*, here, was a symbol for the power of Rome.

*ii*. to provide a legendary explanation for the origin and diversification of languages among peoples. Here the writer, for the purpose of prehistory in Genesis, exploited a legend whose date could not be placed in a prehistoric period. In verse 5 the writer tells of Yahweh coming down to see not what the Babylonians were up to, but what *bᵉn-ey 'adam* "sons of Adam" (i.e., human beings) were up to. This groups the post-deluge story of the confusion of tongues at *Babɛl* with the antediluvian story of the sons of the gods.

*iii*. to provide an etiological explanation for the riddle of the ziggurats of Babylon. Hence the folk etymology of the name *Babɛl*:

> Come, let us go down and *boll-ah* [confuse] their tongue there . . . [Gen. 11:7–8].
>
> Therefore he called its name *Babɛl*
> For there Yahweh *balal* [confused] the speech of the whole earth [Gen. 11:9a].

The intention here is to suggest that there is an etymological relationship between *bbl* and *bll*, which is possible. In this case, however, the folk etymologist is basing etymology on a single leg of sound-similarity without any consideration for the other leg of meaning-similarity. Hebrew *balal* means "mingle, mix, confuse, confound," cognate therefore with the Chi-chewa ideophone *balala-balala* "scatter, disperse." Here etymology has two legs to stand upon: phonology and semantics. But what does *Babɛl* mean?

*Babɛl* is not Hebrew. It is the name of the Babylonian capital whose city gate was memorably designed with religious motifs. It came to be known by the Babylonians as *baab ilu* "the gate of

God" (see Igbo *obube* and Twi *abubuo* "door"; Yoruba *Elú, Olú* "king, God"). *Babɛl*, therefore, could not have been so called because "there Yahweh *balal* the speech of all the world."

The etymologies of Genesis 1–11 are based on fancy, not fact: they serve the purpose of mythology, not that of linguistics or philology. As far as the Genesis writers were concerned, a word in a strange language must connote something similar in a similar-sounding word in Hebrew. The semantic tour de force produces a good story, and in mythology the story is the end. The etymology is simply the means to that end. If, as Helmer Ringgren declares in *Theological Dictionary of the Old Testament, Babɛl* is "neither Sumerian nor Akkadian, and its original meaning is unknown,"[1] we can see how folk etymology came in to fill the gap.

When the Jews were exiled to Babylon in 586 B.C., they were struck by the fact that the Babylonians used *l^e^ben-ah* "brick" (the white limestone variety, not red brick), whereas they used *'ɛbɛn* "stone"; and for plaster the Babylonians used *ḥemɛr* where they used *ḥomɛr*. Subject matter, then, helps to date the story in the period after the Babylonian experience of the Jews. Vocabulary also places the story in this period: Babel was situated in a *biq^e^'ah* "plain" (Yoruba *kpákpá*; cf. Dan. 3:1 and Ezek. 3:22). And the land is called *'ɛrɛṣ šin^e^'ar* "the land of *Shin^e^'ar*."

The story is a comment on political hubris, just as the eating of the fruit of the tree of the knowledge of good and evil is intellectual hubris: the one communal, the other personal. In the one case Yahweh said:

> See! All of them have one council and one language. And yet this is the beginning of what they will do. Now nothing which they take it into their head to do will be out of their reach. Come, let us go down and *ballah* their speech so that one man does not hear the speech of the other [Gen. 11:6–7].

In the other case Yahweh *'^ɛ^loh-iym* said:

> See! the *'adam* has become like one of us (able) to know good and evil. And now, lest he stretch forth his hand and

> takes also of the tree of life and eats and lives forever. . . . And Yahweh *'ɛloh-iym* sent him out of the garden of *'Edɛn* to slave on the soil . . . [Gen. 3:22].

And thus the Hebrew writers reviewed the whole scope of the intellectual, cultural, social, and political adventure of humanity:

| | |
|---|---|
| Adam and *Ḥawwah* | Life or knowledge? |
| *Qayin* and *Hɛbɛl* | Settled agriculture or nomadic pastoralism? Decided by violence. |
| *Qayin* to *Lamɛk* | Technology and the arts. Violence triumphant. |
| Seth and Enosh | Lord have mercy upon us. |
| *hag-gibbor-iym* | Militaristic imperialism leading to the deluge. |
| Noah | Faith and grace: rest. |
| *Babɛl* | Social engineering on a world scale. |

Thus the stage was set for the salvation history beginning with Abram:

> My father was an Aramaean about to perish . . . [Deut. 26:5ff.].

# Epilogue

Some people have designated interpretations that arise from studying the Bible in its original languages "Biblical Studies." They say it is not Bible Study. According to them Bible Study is for devotion, while Biblical Studies are for mere show of learning. My feeling is that if anything is study, it should be *study*. There should be a difference between Bible *study* and Bible *reading*. The eunuch of Ethiopia was reading the Book of the Prophet Isaiah and yet he needed Philip to help him *understand* what he was reading. In Bible reading it is possible to look and look and yet not see, to listen and listen and yet not hear.

Some people say that one does not need knowledge to be able to *understand* the Bible: all one needs is the Holy Spirit. This is turning a "both *(a)* and *(b)*" requirement into an "either *(a)* or *(b)*" alternative. Such people assume that when one has knowledge one automatically loses the Holy Spirit, or that only ignorant people have the gift of the Holy Spirit. Because of such belief, they conclude that all learned interpreters of the Bible are on the road to hell. We leave them with their spirit of ignorance, which makes them prefer superficial appearance to profound significance.

There are legitimate ways of interpreting a passage of Scripture. Genesis 2:7, for instance, reads in the Jerusalem Bible: "Yahweh God fashioned man of dust from the soil. Then he breathed into his nostrils a breath of life, and thus man became a living being." It is illegitimate to jump from here to a conclusion that this shows that human beings are distinct from animals in that the human being has a "soul." Is the "breath of life" (Hebrew *nišᵉm-at ḥayy-iym*; Greek Septuagint *pnoé zōes*) distinctive of human beings? Is the human being the only "living being" (Hebrew *nεfεš ḥayy-ah*; Greek Septuagint *psuche zōsa*)? Are the versions that say ". . . and man became a living soul" justified? (See, e.g., *psuche* in 1 Thess. 5:23.)

In Genesis 1:30 we read of "all the reptiles upon earth in whom is *nɛfɛš ḥayy-ah*" (Greek Septuagint *psuche zōes*). That is, *nɛfɛš ḥayy-ah*, the essence of the human being in Genesis 2:7, is in reptiles too. If *n$^{e}$šam-ah (niš$^{e}$m-at ḥayy-iym: pnoé zōes)* is in the nostrils of human beings (Isa. 2:22a), so is it in the nostrils of animals. Thus we read in Ecclesiastes 3:19–21:

> The *m-qrh* ["fate"] of the sons of Adam and the *m-qrh* of beasts: they have one and the same *m-qrh*. As this dies, so does the other. All have one and the same *ru$^{w}$aḥ* ["breath"]. Take the beast away from the man, the residue is nil. For all is *hɛbɛl*. . . . All took their existence from the dust and all return to the dust. Who knows whether the *ru$^{w}$aḥ* of the sons of Adam does rise up or if the *ru$^{w}$aḥ* of beasts does descend down to the earth?

As both human beings and animals have *n$^{e}$šam-ah*, so do both have *ru$^{w}$aḥ* "wind" » "spirit" (Greek Septuagint *pneuma*). It is not that Ecclesiastes is ignorant of the view that the dust part of human beings (the body) returns to dust while the spirit part *(n$^{e}$šam-ah, ru$^{w}$aḥ)* returns elsewhere. When a *nɛfɛš ḥayy-ah* dies, human or beast, the dust returns to the earth as it was (once), but the *ru$^{w}$aḥ* returns to the gods who gave it (cf. Eccles. 12:7).

| | Hebrew | Greek | Twi | Urhobo | Yoruba | Bini |
|---|---|---|---|---|---|---|
| "animating breath" | *n$^{e}$šam-ah/ru$^{w}$aḥ* | *pnoé/pneu-ma* | *họnhọm* | | | |
| "life, self" | *nɛfɛš/m-qrh* | *psuche* | *kra* | | | |
| | | | *ọ-kra* | | | |
| "destiny" | | | *n-kra-bɛa* | *Ẹrhi* | *orí* | |
| "alter ego" | *ma-l$^{e}$'ak* | *angel-os* (Acts 12:15) | *sunsum* | | | |
| "genius" | *'aḥ-iy 'el* | | | | | *ẹ̀hì* |

If neither *niš$^{e}$m-at ḥayy-iym* (*n$^{e}$šam-ah* in Isa. 2:22) nor *ru$^{w}$aḥ* (*niš$^{e}$m-at ru$^{w}$aḥ ḥayy-iym* in Gen. 7:22) nor *m-qrh* (Twi *n-kra*, *ọ-kra*; Gã *kla* "life principle" metaphysically conceived; Tyo *nkira* "spirit") distinguishes human beings from animals, such a distinction should not be read into Genesis 2:7.

Is there then no difference at all between human beings and animals? Apart from the statement that God gave man *arido* over the animals (Gen. 1:26, 28), which is equivalent to the statement in Genesis 2:19–20 that God brought all the animals to Adam so that he might *qr’* to them (i.e., give them their calling by giving them names), the two creation stories in Genesis do not focus their attention on the difference between human beings and animals. Their concern is the fruitful question "What is man?"—creature or self-generated, autonomous or dependent, blessed or accursed?

The other text that provides an explanation for these questions is Genesis 1:26: "And *’*$^{ɛ}$*loh-iym* said: ‘Let us make *’adam* in our own *ṣɛlɛm*, in our own *d*$^{e}$*m-u*$^{w}$*t*. . . .’ " This text will not add to understanding except one can answer the questions: What is the *ṣɛlɛm* (Greek Septuagint *eikon*) of gods? Is it the same thing as the *d*$^{e}$*m-u*$^{w}$*t* (Greek Septuagint *homoíōsis*[1]) of gods? There is a tendency to equate the two terms: the *eikon* of Caesar on the denarius (Mt. 22:20) is translated into Hebrew as *d*$^{e}$*m-u*$^{w}$*t* (United Bible Societies New Testament *B*$^{e}$*riyt Ḥadašah*). Shall we say that whereas *d*$^{e}$*m-u*$^{w}$*t* is a genetic blood-group likeness, *ṣɛlɛm* is a three-dimensional image?

What does it mean to say that *’adam* was created in *ṣɛlɛm ’*$^{ɛ}$*loh-iym*? The cognates of Hebrew *ṣɛlɛm* in Chadic languages include:

| | | |
|---|---|---|
| Mwaghavul | *čilɛm* | "spirit-double, personality-soul" |
| Pyem | *šulum* | "spirit-double, personality-soul" |

These take us away from physical images of gods, and rightly, too.

"Let us make *’adam* in our own *čilɛm*": Every human being, in this view, has a spiritual double in the spirit world. This spirit-double the Akan call *sunsum* (cf. Twi *sunsuma* "shadow," a reduplication of the Middle Egyptian *snw* "two," and *sn* "brother"). In this view, which is widespread in traditional Africa, every person has a twin in the spirit world, for human beings are created in the *čilɛm* of divine beings. The heavenly *’aḥ* (Hebrew *’aḥ* "brother": Middle Egyptian *ȝh* "beneficent spirit") acts as the guardian angel and the director of the fate of the person on earth. Hence Bini *ẹhì* "guardian angel" and the Hebrew names Ahiel (*’aḥ-iy ’el*—" ’El is my *ẹhì*") and Joah (*Yo ’aḥ*—"Yahweh is *ẹhì*").

Thus in chapter 12 of the Acts of the Apostles we read that when Peter was released from prison in Jerusalem by an angel of the Lord (vs. 11), he went straight to the house of Mary the mother of John Mark. Rhoda, a maid, answered the knock and ran to announce that it was Peter; but they told her that she was out of her mind. When she insisted that it was truly Peter, they said: "It must be his angel" (vs. 15)—the angel of the Lord; the angel of Peter: there is a lot of the primal view of God and human nature that has been subsumed in the biblical category of "angel." An angel of God is the visible manifestation of the invisible God; the angel of Peter is the visible manifestation of Peter when Peter is physically out of sight. The Jerusalem Bible explains that "it was popularly believed that guardian angels were a kind of spiritual 'double' of their charges." The angel of Peter was his *čilɛm*, his *sunsum* "alter ego."

Charismatic personalities who have the power to mesmerize many persons are described in many African idioms as possessing a shadow. Divine beings have a shadow on a very heightened level. Human beings are such *čilɛm* of divine beings. Hence:

> And some divine beings said:
> "Let us make *'adam* in our own *čilɛm*. . . ."

What the divine beings command, the *čilɛm* must carry out; and if the *čilɛm* is to engage in any enterprise it must consult its divine alter ego. For without the support and approval of the divine alter ego, no enterprise of human beings can succeed. Successful human endeavors are the result of a partnership between two persons, the human actor and the spiritual director. One who grieves the spiritual director cannot succeed. For the Hebrew who is named *'aḥ-iy 'el* or *yo 'aḥ* (Joah), Yahweh is the spiritual director.

> According to African dogma sickness and health are ultimately of supernatural origin. . . . Apart from influences external to the patient . . . the patient himself has a *kra* and a *sunsum* (spiritual components of his makeup) . . . whose co-operation is essential for health and prosperity. Further, a bad conscience and ill-will towards others are held to disturb the peace of the indwelling spirit which in turn disturbs the owner's health. Some tribes . . . begin their annual fes-

> tival with a day of peace-making on which people seek out their friends and relatives and confess not only their misdeeds but also any secret resentments they have haboured, holding it useless to ask the gods for health and prosperity when unspoken rancour is gnawing at their vitals.[2]

To show how much our interpretation differs from the current orthodox interpretation of the text, we quote from William Neil's *One Volume Bible Commentary*:

> The Bible sees man, as distinct from the other animals, in a special relationship to God. . . . Whatever the word "image" implies, it certainly means that men in their own sphere are god-like. . . .
>
> But if man alone is made in God's image, human personality has a value which is unique. . . . Above all, the idea of the image of God suggests that there is in man, unlike any other creature, the possibility of responding to God. . . .[3]

We agree that the passage does imply that men are godlike, but we fail to see how one can read from this passage the inference that human beings alone are made in God's image. Monotheism has here been allowed to interfere with the text: once *’ᵋloh-iym* "gods" is rendered into "God," the plural images (bodily manifestations) of plural gods are construed as a singular image of a singular god. Then also *’adam*, who has no human mother, is seen as "human being."

We must correct this last error: human being is *’ᵋnoʷš; ’adam* is not the human being. Adam is the ancestor of human beings. That is why *’ᵋnoʷš* "human being" is called *bɛn ’adam* ("son of *’adam*"). Adam has no human father and no human mother: his father is Yahweh (cf. Fọn *Yɛhwe*, a synonym of *vodũ*, both meaning "divine spirit");[4] his mother is *’adam-ah* "soil." This physical manifestation (image) of divine spirits can be seen in many forms:

| | | |
|---|---|---|
| Yoruba | *Àdàmú òrìṣà* | "the first ancestor" (*ri’š-oʷn ’adam* in Job 15:7) |
| | *àdán* | "the bat" (half mouse, half bird) |
| | *dán* [dã] | "shine, dazzle" (cf. Hebrew *nᵉhoš-ɛt* "bronze") |

| | | |
|---|---|---|
| Fọn | *Dã* | "the snake spirit, the guardian spirit"; *Dã* revealing himself as a snake (cf. Hebrew *nahaš* "serpent") |
| Yoruba | *ẹdun* | "white colobus monkey" (totem of twins) |
| Gã | *adun* | "red patas monkey" |
| Twi | *odum* | *Chlorophora excelsa* (a tree spirit) |
| Igbo, Bini | *odum* | "lion" (powerful tawny animal) |
| Swahili | *duma* | "cheetah" (powerful animal, the fastest of all animals) |
| Ijọ | *odum* | "python" (a water spirit) |

Who says, then, that *'adam* in Genesis 1:26 means "human being"? For "human being" we must go to the phrase *'adam yᵉluʷd 'iššah* ("the *'adam* born of woman") in Job 14:1. The implication is that there are *'adam* who are not born of woman. One such is *ri'š-oʷn 'adam* "the first of *'adam*," the first of the double-natured beings who, like *àdán* "the bat," are of two species—of the earth and of the air, dust and spirit. The necessary characteristic of *'adam* is "strength," muscular power beyond that which is normal in human beings. Who would say that a lion or a python or an *ìrókò* tree does not qualify for the title *'adam*?

William Neil deduces from the thesis of the uniqueness of human beings that "men and women may not be treated as goods and chattels or as cogs in a machine or as tools of the state." Many African people traditionally respected the status of pythons and *ìrókò* trees as *'adam* created in *ṣɛlɛm 'ᵋloh-iym*. With this theological basis for such "animism," Africans simply did not cut down *odum* trees. Without such a theology, on what basis do people who eliminate the most intelligent of the animals from the category of *'adam* legislate for the preservation of some of the species from extinction? And how can they tell human beings, if they alone are made in God's image, to

> Go to the ant, thou sluggard.
> Consider her ways and be wise.

We cannot have a comprehensive *ṣɛlɛm 'ᵋloh-iym* by eliminating all the living things in whose presence we feel an unmistakable *numen tremendum*. Here is the Kalahari Bushman view of "Our Other Person":

> A man has died.
> We say that he
> is now another person,
> and we respect
> the one who has
> become our other person.
>
> And when we see
> a snake upon
> his grave, we do not touch it.
> We do not kill
> the snake because
> that snake is our dead person. . . .
>
> We show respect,
> we do not kill
> that which has been a man
> for both the snake
> and lizard are
> the dead man's other person.[5]

Thomas Berry writes:

> The intercommunion of life systems, understood with a certain instinctive awareness by tribal peoples throughout the world, is something that the white man, with all his science and technology, seems unable to appreciate, even when his very existence is imperilled. European man has had a certain sense of himself as above all other living things, as the absolute lord and master of the earth. He sees the earth as divinely presented to him to do with as he pleased. . . . The earth, it seemed, would bear any amount of human exploitation, would sustain any amount of damage. . . . With a supreme shock the white man discovers that the earth is a delicate balance of life systems, that the fuels for his machines are limited, that defacing the earth defiles man and destroys the divine voice that speaks so powerfully through every phase of cosmic activity.

> The Indian now offers to the Euroamerican a mystical sense of the place of the human amid other living beings.[6]

In the Christian Aid pamphlet *World Development and the Bible,* Eric Jay writes that Genesis 1, Psalm 8, Isaiah 65:17–25, and Revelation 21 show that the Hebrews at an early stage broke away from one of the oldest religious beliefs in the world—the belief that rocks and streams, forests and hills are dwelling places of gods and demons and that certain animals and birds are sacred.

> In Hebrew belief, man is set free from the tyranny of nature; he is liberated from magic and superstition. He need not be afraid of his environment. His role is to "have dominion" in that environment, to manipulate and use it creatively for his own good. . . . The river, for example, no longer has any religious status for him.

No wonder . . . no wonder you can no longer catch fish in the river Rhine, and can no longer swim in it without danger to your life. The Hebrew belief without which "the rise of modern science and technology would have been impossible" has turned the Rhine into a sewage pipe of industrial poison. Who says that human beings "need not reverence it as being the home of spirits"? Only those who are no longer capable of comprehending what ancient wisdom called "spirits." Theologians ought not to betray such ignorance. To read into Genesis 1:26 a doctrine that "man alone is made in God's image" is to open the way for human beings to play God in the ecological environment, to use (to "manipulate") nature instead of nurturing it.

When you narrow the domain of the spiritual, the sacred, and the sacramental (from many divine spirits believed to be manifested in many botanical and zoological forms to a single divine spirit believed to be manifested in one zoological form), you need go only one more step from monotheism to find that the awareness of the spiritual, the sacred, and the sacramental is snuffed out of human experience. You are left with materialism and secularism as intellectual human beings dominate nature and exploit it as mere material—creating, inevitably, ecological blight.

# Appendix

## I. Nimrod

Although we are here concerned solely with Nimrod the mythological hero, and not with Nimrod-Nimrud the city (i.e., Nineveh); with the ancestry of Nimrod, and not with the location of Nimrud, it might nevertheless be appropriate to quote M. E. L. Mallowan on Nimrud.

> It may seem surprising that many persons who are familiar with the name Nineveh, the most famous city of Assyria, have hardly heard of Nimrud and would find it difficult to define. Indeed, until recently there were some authorities on Old Testament studies who thought that these two places were synonymous. Perhaps the comprehensive publication in 1966 of *Nimrud and its Remains* has helped to set Nimrud in its proper perspective. . . .
>
> It is, however, not only historically that the memory of the place has been clouded, but philologically also. Nimrud, correctly pronounced Nimrood, is often casually referred to as Nimrod . . . partly because from the Old Testament we retain a memory of Gen.X.9—"Like Nimrod a mighty hunter before the Lord," whereas Nimrud itself is never mentioned. Yet we may not be wrong in connecting these two not altogether dissimilar names. . . . Nimrud . . . was eventually assimilated to Nimrod of the Old Testament and the mythological hero associated with Abraham in the Koran.
>
> The strange genealogy is fortified in its relation to the ancient site by a passage in Gen.X.1–12 where the hero is associated with the city: . . .

The names Nimrod and Calah have been italicized in order to emphasize the connection between the two, a real one, although the author of this passage in Genesis may hardly have been aware of it. . . .

We have already seen that the equation of Nimrod-Nimrud is philologically acceptable, and to these may be added Calah, for this is obviously the Old Testament name for Assyrian Kalhu. . . .[1]

The section on "*Nim*$^{e}$*rod*, The First Emperor" (pp. 25ff.) is an attempt to interpret Genesis 10:1–8a:

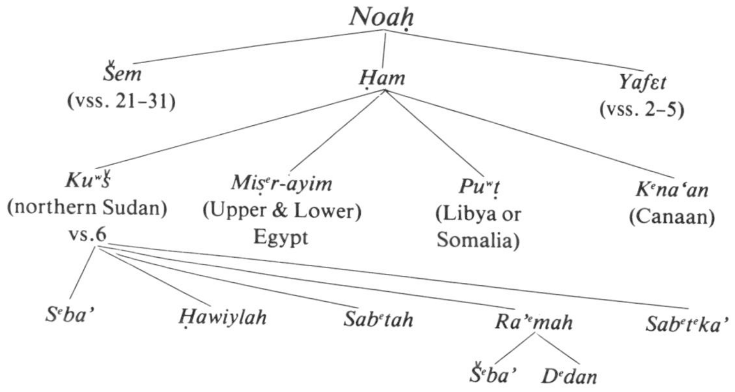


Is *Ku*$^{w}$*š* in Genesis 10:6a the same as *Ku*$^{w}$*š* in Genesis 10:8a—"And *Ku*$^{w}$*š* gave birth to Nimrod"? E. A. Speiser writes:

Cush. This geographic term is used in the Bible for two widely separated lands whose names happen to be similar by coincidence: (1) Ethiopia, as [in Gen. 10:6a]. (2) Cossaea, the country of the Kassites, as in vs. 8 . . . and Genesis 2:13.[2]

. . . The chaotic geography of ancient and modern exponents of this biblical text can be traced largely to two factors. One is the mistaken identification of the land of Cush [in Gen. 2:13 and 10:8] with the homonymous biblical term for Ethiopia, rather than with the country of the Kassites; note the spelling *Kuššũ* in the Nuzu documents, and the classical Gr. form Kossaios.[3]

Does this solve the problem of the *Ku*$^{w}$*š* in verse 8?

Let us take the *Ku*$^{w}$*š* of verse 6, the son of Ham, whom all authorities agree is Ethiopia, more accurately northern Sudan: *(i)* his "brothers" include Canaan, considered by modern linguistic classification to be a Semite; *(ii)* his sons are all Semites according to modern linguistic classification; *(iii)* one set of his "grandsons" (*S*$^{e}$*ba'* and *D*$^{e}$*dan*) are Arabians and therefore Semites according to modern linguistic classification.

What, then, shall we say? That the writer of the biblical text was mixed up about the ethnic classification of *Ku*$^{w}$*š* even in Genesis 10:6–7? Was he not saying, in effect, that there are many peoples, today grouped as Semites, who in his view *descended from* the area of northern Sudan and Ethiopia? Is this different from his statement that *Ku*$^{w}$*š* gave birth to Nimrod, identified by archeologists to be in Assyria?

A. N. Tucker, in the paper "What's in a Name?" that he delivered to the Colloquium on Hamito-Semitic Comparative Linguistics in London in March 1970, said:

> The choice of Cush as the father of a language group was not a very happy one when it is remembered that Accadian is also a Semitic language of Asia Minor, in spite of the relationship of Accad to Nimrod, son of Cush!
>
> Some adjustment was evidently called for just at a period in our history when the Bible was coming in for increased criticism as the ultimate historical authority. But the overall unity of these languages was recognised at an early date—hence the term "Semito-Hamitic" or "Hamito-Semitic." . . . This overall unity did not apparently extend to Noah's third son and his descendants. . . .
>
> In recent years the feeling has grown in linguistic circles . . . that the linguistic criteria for dividing the Semitic and Hamitic languages into two distinctive blocks does not exist. All these languages have certain common elements in vocabulary, morphemes and patterns of grammatical behaviours (especially in verb conjugation), which are characteristic of the whole family.[4]

J. H. Greenberg, writing on "Language, Diffusion and Migration," says:

> Related languages are likely to be in the same geographical region but usually are not in continuous distribution. In principle, geography is irrelevant, although it is a normal result that related languages are in the same general area. This is a reflection of the types of population movements which have in fact occurred in the past.[5]

And Edward Ullendorf writes in *Ethiopia and the Bible*:

> The people [of Ethiopia] . . . constitute an amalgam of Hamites, Semites and Nilotic groups. Whether the Cushitic (i.e., Hamitic Ethiopian) peoples originally came from southern Arabia, whence the Hamito-Semites may have sprung, or whether the cradle of the once united Hamito-Semitic race was—as some scholars have conjectured—in that part of Africa which is now called Ethiopia, need not concern us at present. In any event, the prolonged influx of Semitic elements from south-west Arabia, in pre-Christian centuries and later, has once again brought about a union of Hamites and Semites. The stage is the Abyssinian plateau where the result of this renewed fusion has been the emergence of the Hamites as the predominant ethnic factor and of the Semites as the principal linguistic and cultural element.[6]

Of the two theories of the origin of the Hamito-Semites (southern Arabia or Ethiopia), the biblical statement that *Ku*$^{w}$*š* is the father of *S*$^{e}$*ba'*, *Ḥawiylah*, *Sab*$^{e}$*tah*, *Ra'*$^{e}$*mah*, and *Sab*$^{e}$*t*$^{e}$*ka'* and the grandfather of *Š*$^{e}$*ba* and *D*$^{e}$*dan* supports the second theory. "Where Semitic origins in particular are concerned, an African source seems likely," writes B. S. J. Isserling.[7] It is this that makes the present author see no problem in Genesis 10:8a, "*Ku*$^{w}$*š* gave birth to Nimrod," particularly when the legendary hero Nimrod is known in Yoruba legend as *Lámúrúdù*.

The text we are trying to interpret is not a historical text: its mythical mode allows it to convey ideological assumptions (like the Hebrew denial of kinship with the Canaanites). How does one offer a pertinent interpretation of ideological assumptions? To what extent is verifiable historical evidence pertinent? Are place-names always explainable from historical events and geographical circumstances, or do ideological assumptions also play a part? Where is Eden? Where is the land of Nod? Where is the city that *Tubal Qayin* built and named after his son *Ḥano*$^{w}$*k*? Are these problems for archeology (history) alone or are they also problems of myth and legend (of ideology and communal belief)?

When it is said, for instance, that "The Canaanites are Semitic, not black," this writer would say of the first part of the statement: "Yes, but the Hebrew writers of Genesis 10 did not think so." What they *thought* was that the Canaanites were not Semites but Hamites. Which opinion, then, is it necessary to interpret—their ideological views or the modern scientific view? And concerning the statement "And *Ku*$^{w}$*š* gave birth to Nimrod" (Gen. 10:8a), is this the archeological Nimrud or "the mythological hero associated with Abraham in the Koran"?

We quote from Samuel Johnson, *The History of the Yorubas*:

> That the Yorubas came originally from the East there cannot be the slightest doubt, as their habits, manners and customs . . . all go to prove. With them the East is Mecca and Mecca is the East. Having strong affinities with the East, and Mecca in the East looming so largely in their imagination, everything that comes from the East, with them, comes from Mecca, and hence it is natural to represent themselves as having hailed originally from that city.
>
> The only written record we have on this subject is that of the Sultan Belo of Sokoto, . . . the most learned . . . of the Fulani sovereigns that ever bore rule in the Soudan. . . . Yarba is an extensive province containing rivers, forests, sands and mountains. . . .
>
> The inhabitants of this province (Yarba) it is supposed originated from the remnant of the children of Canaan, who were of the tribe of Nimrod. The cause of their establishment in the West of Africa was, as it is stated, in consequence of their being driven by Yarrooba, son of Kahtan, out of Arabia to the Western Coast between Egypt and Abyssinia. From that spot they advanced into the interior of Africa, till they reached Yarba where they fixed their residence. . . .

> In the name Lamurudu (or Namurudu) we can easily recognise a dialectic modification of the name Nimrod. Who this Nimrod was, whether Nimrod surnamed "the strong," the son of Hasoul, or Nimrod the "mighty hunter" of the Bible, we cannot tell. Arabia is probably the "Mecca" of our tradition. It is known that the descendants of Nimrod (Phoenicians) were led in war to Arabia. . . .[8]

This extract is to be read in the context of the whole section, which begins: "The origin of the Yoruba nation is involved in obscurity. Like the early history of most nations the commonly received accounts are for the most part purely legendary."[9]

The *Lámúrúdù* of the Yoruba legend of origin, then, is "the mythological hero associated with Abraham in the Koran." The genealogical phraseology of Genesis 10:8a leaves this writer in no doubt that the passage is legendary, ideological, subjective. Stories of the same hero may have spread to Mesopotamia, to Arabia, to Yorubaland. How else do we have the grave of the Queen of Sheba (known in Arabic as *Bilqis* = Yoruba *Bìrìkísù Sùnm̀gbọ́*) at Oke Ẹri, forty-one miles from Ibadan, Nigeria, and three miles from Ijẹbu Ode? The explanation may be simply Muslim travelers' tales, but the grave is now preserved as one of Nigeria's national monuments. And if we can easily trace Yoruba *Bìrìkísù* from the Arabic *Bilqis*, what about the older Yoruba doublet of *bìrìkísù*—Yoruba *kpanṣágà* "adultery": Hebrew *piylɛgɛš̌* "concubine" (» Greek *pallaké* "concubine"), which points to the fact that *Bilqis* was considered to be a concubine of Solomon?

Myths and legends do travel with people. And if a city—Nimrud in Mesopotamia—is named after a mythological hero, Nimrod, we cannot assume that the name of the city is the first occurrence of the name. Herman Gunkel writes in *The Legends of Genesis*:

> To us it seems probable from interior evidence that these legends wandering from race to race reached Canaan as early as some time in the second millennium B.C. and were adopted by Israel just as it was assimilating the civilization of Canaan. . . .[10]

> . . . theologians should learn that Genesis is not to be understood without the aid of the proper methods for the study of legends.[11]

"And *Ku*$^{w}$*š* gave birth to Nimrod." Archeology has located this Nimrod in a place-name in Mesopotamia: the vagaries of mythology have produced stories of Nimrod in Arabia and in Yorubaland. What, really, is the conflict? The conflict is between the archeologist and the mythologist. The fact that the archeologist in Mesopotamia shouts, "*Eureka!* I have found Nimrod in the ruins of Nimrud" does not prevent the Yoruba from shouting, "*Eureka!* We have found the *Lámúrúdù* of our legend of origin in the Nimrod of Genesis 10:8"—particularly when the Nimrod of Genesis 10:8 is called in Hebrew a *gibbo*$^{w}$*r* "strong man," which the Yoruba language immediately matches with the word *alágbára* "possessor of power."

The legend is not a fake: it is as real as the ruins of Nimrud. The archeologist would like an opportunity to dig into the grave of *Bìrìkísù Sùnǹgbọ́* at Oke Ẹri to prove or disprove the Yoruba belief that there the Queen of Sheba was buried. But that would be desecration—plucking from the fruit of the knowledge of good and evil! Neither the people of Oke Ẹri nor the Nigerian Antiquities Commission would permit that. We think they are right.

## II. YHWH

It is not as sacrilegious as it may seem at first to point out a cognate relationship between YHWH in the Old Testament and Fọn *Yɛhwe*, Ewe *Yèvè* "spirit," "la Puissance de la Foudre."[12] After all, Hebrew *qo*$^{w}$*l* in *qo*$^{w}$*l YHWH* "the voice of YHWH" (Ps. 29) has a cognate in Igbo *Kalu*, the divinity of thunder, the "god" of retribution whom the Igbo also know as *Kamalu* (:YHWH is *'el g*$^{e}$*mul-o*$^{w}$*t, g*$^{e}$*mu*$^{w}$*l* in Jeremiah 51:56b and 51:6b). The Hebrews did know of the conception of YHWH as the *'ɛl* whose *qo*$^{w}$*l* makes the lightning flash, just as the Fọn of Dahomey (the Republic of Benin) know *Yɛhwe* to be "la Puissance de la Foudre."

Robert H. Pfeiffer states:

> The name *Yahweh* in the Semitic dialect spoken by the Kenites must have had a meaning and thus characterized the deity. If we could discover this meaning we would have a good idea of the original character of this god. But the efforts of modern scholars, who have suggested numerous etymologies of this name, have failed to supply a convincing solution to the mystery. The word belongs to a lost language.
>
> Nor does Ex. 3:14 supply a clue to the meaning. . . . None of the sources of the Pentateuch had the slightest inkling of what "Yahweh" meant originally.[13]

The reason why we think that Fọn *Yɛhwe*, "la Puissance de la Foudre," offers an insight into the original meaning of YHWH is that the tie *YHWH:Yɛhwe* is not isolated coincidence. All the other Old Testament names of God are reflected in this area of West Africa:

| | | | | | |
|---|---|---|---|---|---|
| Hebrew | *’ɛl* | "God" | :Yoruba | *Elú/Olú* | "God" |
| | *’*$^{\varepsilon}$*loah(’lh)* | "God" | :Yoruba | *Olúwa* | "lord, master, God" (*-l-w-*) |
| | *’el šadday* | | :Jukun | *tsido* | "God" |
| | *’el ‘ɛl*$^{e}$*y-o*$^{w}$*n* | "topmost, | | | |
| | *‘ɛl*$^{e}$*y-o*$^{w}$*n* | highest" | :Efik | *enyoz* | "top, peak" |

Is YHWH in the Hebrew Scriptures always translatable as "God" (the God of the Hebrews)? The question would not have arisen if we did not have the problematic passage in Genesis 4:1—"I have acquired a man *’ɛt YHWH*." Could *Ḥawwah* be saying, "I have acquired a man and God"?

The versions that have "I have acquired a man *with the help of God*" are not translating Hebrew *’ɛt*, which is either "and, with" or the particle preceding the direct object. Because the resultant version would present a problem of meaning, they make "with the help of" out of *’ɛt* "with" (:Yoruba *àti* "with").

Now, if one dropped the idea that YHWH always means "God" and applies the fact that Fọn *Yɛhwe*, Ewe *Yèvè* mean "divine spirit,"[14] then one has an alternative (philological) method of making sense out of an otherwise problematic passage.

## III. The Sin of Ham and the Curse on Canaan

The problem raised by Genesis 9:22–26 is that the curse on Canaan (vss. 25–26) seems not to be directed at the culprit; for it was not Canaan who saw the nakedness of Noah and did nothing about it. It was Ham.

Perhaps the description of Ham as "Ham the father of Canaan" helps us to see how the seeming error occurred: it is undeniable that the story was intended to portray Ham as lacking in filial responsibility. If the story ends with the seeming non sequitur of the curse on Canaan, it merely shows that the Hebrew writers had an ax to grind not only with Ham and not only with Canaan but with both of them together.

We begin to see why the Hebrew writers denied kinship with the Canaanites and sought for them an ancestry different from their own. The criterion here seems to be attitude to strong drink: all the children of Ham, being agriculturalists, were indulgent toward strong drink whereas the children of Shem, being shepherds, tended to maintain an ascetic stance toward strong drink.

E. A. Speiser's statement in *Genesis* that "The apparent purpose of this remark [Ham being the father of Canaan] is to relate Ham to the subsequent curse against Canaan, . . . to telescope Ham and Canaan, as is now the case"[15] is deliberate anti-Hamitism. This is what John B. Thompson calls *split reference*: "The mobilisation of meaning in order to sustain relations of domination [which] commonly involves . . . a splitting of the referential domain. The terms of a discourse carry out their ideological role by explicitly referring to one thing and implicitly referring to another, by entangling these multiple referents in a way which serves to sustain relations of domination."[16]

If, as some contend, the oracle refers to David and Solomon in their subjugation of the Canaanite or if, as the *Encyclopaedia Judaica* says:

> This could only fit the period of the Conquest when Israel, under Joshua's leadership, invaded and conquered the land of Canaan at the same time that the people known to the

> writer of the passage as "the children of Japheth," namely, the nations of the Mediterranean islands (Gen. 10:2, 4, 5), also attacked and conquered the land, as recorded in the accounts of the invasions of the . . . inscriptions of Pharaoh Merneptah (c. 1230 B.C.E.),[17]

why not leave Ham entirely out of it?

We are asked not to believe that the Canaanites have any relationship to the sons of *Ku*$^{w}$*š* through Ham, and yet the *ba*$^{ʿa}$*l-iym* of the Canaanites are the *lu-baale* of the Baganda against whom the crusading zeal of Christianity, Commerce, and Civilization was directed in the late nineteenth century.[18] The *k-r-m* root in Hebrew *kɛrɛm* "vineyard," *kar*$^{e}$*m-ɛl* "wooded hill" is the *k-l-m* in Swahili *kilimo* "agriculture" and in the name of the highest mountain in Africa: *Kilima Njaro*.

We must point out here the sterility of a historical interpretation of an ideological passage. History is that which happened in the past; an ideology is meant to have the ability of resurrecting and giving birth to subsequent histories. We know that the belief that Ham was the father of Canaan mirrors accurately Hebrew ideology, however much it may be incorrect according to modern linguistic classification. It is the same ideology that prevented the Hebrew writers from leaving Ham out of a curse meant for Canaan. It is the business of blacks to expose the inherent anti-Hamitism, which resulted in the paradigmatic extermination of the Canaanites by those who, when the tide turned, have been complaining about anti-Semitism. We are asked not to believe that the *Abore* have any relationship with the *ʿib*$^{e}$*r-iym*; and yet what the *ʿib*$^{e}$*r-iym* did to the Canaanites in the name of Yahweh the *Abore* have done to the sons of *Ku*$^{w}$*š* from Sokoto to Ilorin in the name of Allah.

The *Encyclopaedia Judaica* explains that

> according to the critics "Ham the father of" in Gensis 9:22 may be a gloss; it was Canaan who committed the misdeed, and who is meant by Noah's "youngest son" in verse 24, and consequently it is Canaan who is cursed in verses 25–27. "Ham being the father of Canaan" (9:18b), too, would in that case also be a gloss added to connect verses 18–19 with verses 20, 27.[19]

Glosses are deliberate insertions, not scribal errors. An interpreter cannot ignore their implications.

## IV. The *'Apiru*

Some scholars believe the *'Apiru* not to have been wandering nomads. Others, however, take a different view. Norman Gottwald has the following entries in his glossary in *A Light to the Nations*:

**Apiru.** Egyptian equivalent of Habiru and cognate of Hebrew.[20]

**Habiru.** Semitic seminomadic freebooters and mercenaries, active in the Fertile Crescent in the second millennium; the term is cognate with Hebrew; see also Apiru.[21]

**Hebrew.** (Heb. "one who crosses over, an immigrant, a transient.") (1) A Semitic descendant of Eber, including Israelites, Arabs, Edomites, Moabites, and Ammonites. (2) The people of Israel in the preëxilic period, in contrast to postexilic Jew. . . .[22]

Roland de Vaux writes in *The Early History of Israel*: "In some texts, the 'Apiru are portrayed as settled people, but others describe them as having been nomadic or as still leading this kind of existence."[23]

Siegfried Herrmann writes in *Israel in Egypt*:

> Scholars have up to now been virtually unanimous in the view that the Old Testament *'ibri* must be identical with the *hapiru* or *habiru* and with the Egyptian *'pr*, plural *'pr-w*. . . . In view of the philological identity of the word (which is hardly open to dispute), it seemed an obvious conjecture that a more or less identical phenomenon, relating to groups of people, was to be understood. Now . . . it seems more likely that this was a name for people living under particular conditions, perhaps people accustomed to a nomadic life.

> The opinion therefore came to be widely accepted that the expression ought correctly to be interpreted sociologically, and that it covered particular non-established elements. . . .[24]

Here we are already introduced into the second point of controversy among scholars about the *'Apiru*: that the word refers to a sociological class and not to an ethnic group.

George V. Pixley, in *God's Kingdom*, agrees with the view that the *'Apiru* are a sociological class:

> *'Apiru* appears, then, to have been a sociological term rather than an ethnic one. *'Apiru* were any group that placed itself outside the law and sought its interests by means which were not acceptable to the constituted authorities.
>
> . . . It is this situation of civil unrest that provided the conditions for the emergence of such a tribal, antimonarchical nation as Israel.[25]

The problem with this way of explaining the *'Apiru* phenomenon is: How did a far-flung sociological class become known over a wide area by words that are philologically identical? What is the social (human) background of the wide dispersion of the philologically related terms? And how does a tribe (Israel) emerge from a nonethnic sociological class? A study of sedentarization among the Fulani nomads of West Africa shows how nomads attack settlements and take over power when opportunity offers. It happened in ancient Ghana; it happened in Mali; it happened in Songhai. The last such occurrence was the *jihad* of Uthman dan Fodio through which the Fulani took over the government of the Hausa states in Nigeria in the nineteenth century.

Roman Jakobson refers to "the striking dialectical homogeneity of nomads' languages."[26] He says that this homogeneity "bears obvious relationship to the wide radius of nomadic roaming." The observation is pertinent here: the reflexes of the word *'pr* were widespread in the Middle East; the Fulani nomads of West Africa speak the same language from the Gambia and Senegal to the Cameroon. The linguistic homogeneity indicates in both cases nomadic roaming.

Roland de Vaux devotes many pages of *The Early History of Israel* to raising objections to "the most common view . . . that the name [*'Apiru*] applies not to a people, nation or ethnic group with a particular geographical location, but rather to a class of individuals." He continues:

> They all presuppose that these people were called by a nickname "fugitives," "receivers of rations" or the "dusty" people and that they did not call themselves by any such name. It is, however, very unlikely that the same nickname was given and maintained for almost a millennium in many different regions and by people speaking different languages even when this name no longer applied to their way of life or to their activities at that time. . . .
>
> These difficulties are eliminated as soon as we cease to think of the 'Apiru as a class in society and regard them as a people. . . . Some documents suggest that the word Habiru should be applied to an ethnic group and others almost compel us to accept this interpretation. . . . [27]

The map on p. 65 links (*i*) the area of attestation of the *Sa-Gaz Habiru*, the *Habiru*, the *'apr-m*, the *'ib$^e$r-iym* and the *'pr-w* all over the Fertile Crescent from southern Mesopotamia to the Nile Delta with (*ii*) the area of the attested migration of the *Pulo*, the *Ful-be*, the *Abore*, and the *Bororo* in the West African savannah from Senegambia to the Cameroon. The guides for this link are the following (*i*) the *'pr-w* could not have gone underground in the Middle East just because their mention vanished from written records; (*ii*) the *Pulo/Abore* could not have emerged from the ground in Senegambia in the tenth century A.D. and commenced an eastward nomadic migration that has not yet ended; (*iii*) there is a ground link as much as a philological link between the Middle East set of terms (*Habiru*, *'pr-w*, etc.) and the West African set of terms (*Pulo*, *Abore*, *Bororo*).

For those who insist that there could have been no such movement of peoples through Egypt because there are no records of it in Egypt, we ask: Do there have to be records of it in Egypt before we can deduce it? J. B. Callender writes:

> Orientalists have always been keenly aware that the languages of antiquity represent the main source of our knowl-

edge about ancient cultures. Where no written records are available, we know little indeed, in spite of the valiant efforts of archaeologists. The grammarian is responsible for the decipherment and correct understanding of the relevant languages, and thus the state of linguistic research is, in a certain sense, the touchstone of the discipline as a whole.[28]

". . . How can *habiru* or *'apiru* be related to *ìbhᵉrî*?" asks Roland de Vaux. And he answers:

This is not insurmountable. . . . The Akkadian transcription *habiru* was imperfect and the Ugaritic and Egyptian forms of the word show that the initial consonant was *'ain*. On the basis of the same evidence, the middle consonant was -p-, but an alteration between -p- and -b- was fairly frequent in Ugaritic itself or between Ugaritic and other Semitic languages including Hebrew. . . .[29]

For readers of *The Sons of the Gods* who are interested in knowing, the arguments in this book arise out of the following established equations:

Hebrew *Qayin* (Arabic *qayn* "smith," *quyun* "smiths") has cognates in
- Yoruba *Ògún*, Fọn *Gún* "patron saint of iron workers"
- Hahm (Jaba) *Kuno* "the inventor of iron smelting"
- Ebira *Egene* "the caste of smiths"

Hebrew *Ḥawwah* has cognates in
- Yoruba *ùwà*, *ìwà* "existence, life" (from *wà* "to exist")
- Igbo *uwa* "world, life"
- Hausa *uwa* "mother"
- Jukun *wuwa* "woman"

Hebrew *'adam* has cognates in
- Awori Yoruba *Àdàmú* (*Adamu Òrìṣà* = Hebrew *ri'š̌-oʷn 'adam*)
- Yoruba *àdán* "the bat" (cf. Hebrew *tam*: Yoruba *tán* "finished")
- Igbo *odum* "lion"
- Ijọ *odum* "python"
- Fọn *dã* "python"

Twi *odum* "the *ìrókò* tree," *Chlorophora excelsis* (cf. Hebrew *’rk* "tall")

Hebrew *’$^{\varepsilon}$no$^{w}$š* "human being" has cognates in

Igbo *onye* "person of" (cf. Hebrew construct state *’on$^{e}$š-ey* "persons of")

Bantu *nya-* "person of" (e.g., *Ba-nya-nkole* "plural-persons of-Nkole," *Ba-nya-Rwanda*, etc.)

Yoruba *ònìy-àn* "human being"

Yoruba *ènìy-àn* "human being" (cf. Arabic *’in$^{e}$s-aan* "human being")

Hebrew *ḥay* "living being" has cognates in

Yoruba *ayé* "life, world"

Yoruba *iye* "mother"

Yoruba *ìyè* "survival" (from *yè* "to survive, to live through")

Yoruba *Ẹ̀yọ̀* "the dead come back to life"

Yoruba *ọ̀yà* "(bush) animal" (cf. Hebrew *ḥayy-at has-sadɛh*)

Hebrew *g$^{e}$bu$^{w}$r-ah* "strength," *gibbo$^{w}$r* "strong man" have cognates in

Yoruba *agbára* "power, strength"

Yoruba *al-ágbára* "possessor of power" (cf. Hebrew *g$^{e}$bu$^{w}$l* "boundary": Yoruba *àgbàlá* "courtyard fenced round," Igbo *ikpele* "boundary")

Hebrew *gan* "garden," *ganan* "to fence round" have cognates in

Hausa *gona* "farm"

Yoruba *ẹgàn* "bush, virgin forest"

Yoruba *ìgànná* "wall, fence"

Hebrew *‘edɛn* "luxury, dainty, delight," *ma-‘$^{a}$dan* "dainty (food), delight" have cognates in

Yoruba *dùn* "be delicious"

Yoruba *mùdùnmúdùn* "sweet dainties"

(Even the homophonous Hebrew word *‘edɛn* [see Assyrian *edinu*] "plain" is matched in Yoruba by *ọ̀dàn* "grassland, savannah plain")

Hebrew *yo$^{w}$m (ywm)* "day," *yo$^{w}$man* "by day" have cognates in

Itsekiri *ejuma* "tomorrow morning"

Yoruba *ojúmọ́* "day" (cf. *ojojúmọ́* "every day" « *ojú-mọ́ojúmọ́*: Hebrew *yo$^{w}$myo$^{w}$m* "every day"

Yoruba *ojúmọmọ* "broad daylight" (Hebrew *ywmm*)

Hebrew *layl-ah* "night" is Yoruba *alẹ́lẹ́, alẹ́* "night"
Hebrew *'o$^w$r* "light" is Yoruba *òwúrọ̀* "morning" (Yoruba *wúrà* "gold" is from the same root)
Hebrew *bara'* "to begin" is Yoruba *bẹ̀rẹ̀* "to begin"
Hebrew *bo$^w$re'* "creator" is Twi *Borebore* "creator"
Hebrew *mab-bu$^w$l* "downpour" is Chichewa *m-vula*; Bemba *m-fula* "rain"
Hebrew *m$^e$t-u$^w$* "man of . . .," *m$^e$t-ey* "men of . . ." is Igbo *madu* "human being," *ndi* "people of . . .," *ndu* "life"; Swahili *mtu* "human being"
Hebrew *gaḥo$^w$n* "belly" (of reptiles)" is Yoruba *ikùn* "belly"
Assyrian *giḫinnu* "cord" is Yoruba *okùn* "rope, cord"
Hebrew *yada'* "to know" (imperative masculine singular *da'*), the use of which in the Hebrew idiom "to know a woman" E. A. Speiser says is "not a matter of delicate usage,"[30] is Yoruba *dó* "to copulate"
Hebrew *gawa'* "he died," *yi-g$^e$wa'* "he will die" is Idoma *kwú* "die"; Yoruba *kú* "die," *yíóò kú* "he will die"
Hebrew *ṭḥr* "to be pure" is Twi *dwira* "purify"; Yoruba *tòrò* "clean"
Hebrew *ṭ$^e$ḥor-ah* "purification" is Twi *Odwira* "festival of purification"
Hebrew *p$^e$riy* "fruit" is Igbo *m-kpuru* "fruit"; Efik *mfri* "flower"
Hebrew *p$^e$riy 'eṣ* "fruit of a tree" is Igbo *mkpuru osisi* "fruit of a tree"

These are the fixed beacons from which we venture to speculate about toponymy: *(i)* that Hebrew *Ḥano$^w$k* is Hahm *Nok* (cf. Hebrew *ḥazaq* "be strong": Hausa *zákì* "lion"); *(ii)* that Hebrew *Nod* is Yoruba *Oǹdó*; *(iii)* that Hebrew *Ku$^w$š̌* is Yoruba *Kòso*. Carleton Hodge has spoken of the "very tentative state of affairs within Afroasiatic":

> We do not yet know precisely what languages belong to the group or the precise relationships of the given groups to each other. Speculation regarding even broader ties is to be welcomed, but only if it takes advantage of latest developments and fully recognises the very tenuous character of its conclusions.[31]

There is something called the "informed guess." For our suggestion that the land of *Nod* to which the writer of Gen. 4:16 said *Qayin* (= *Ògún*) went out to dwell, we offered the information about the convergence of the veneration of *Ògún* as the patron divinity of iron workers and the prevalence of *Akin* "valiant man" (Middle Egyptian *qny* "elite corps") in the personal names of Yoruba from Ondo. It is not that we are ignorant of the fact that the name of the land of *Nod* is a play on words from Hebrew *nadad* "to wander, to flutter" (cf. Hebrew *no*$^{w}$*ded kanaf* "flutterer of wings"—a bird—with Yoruba *al-ákpá ǹdẹ̀dẹ̀* "the swallow," where Hebrew *kanaf*, *kapp-* "wing" is Yoruba *akpá* "arm, wing"). It is the same convergence of iron working (*Qayin* and *Kuno*) and the family of *Qayin* in the name of the first city, *Ḥano*$^{w}$*k*, that suggests the earliest civilization of the central Sudan, *Nok*, as the reflex of *Ḥano*$^{w}$*k*.[32] The suggestion that *Kòso* of the *Ọba Kòso* legend is *Ku*$^{w}$*š̌* is offered as an alternative to the folk etymology current among the Yoruba (see pp. 28–30, above). We believe that in these three onomastic speculations we are not prospecting without fixed coordinates.

The children of *Qayin* whom we try to trace to Nok and Ondo are simply descendants of the smith (*Qayin*, *Ògún*, *Kuno*). They could also be found among the *Egene*, "the caste of despised smiths who do iron working over a wide area of Igbirra country in Nigeria." Smiths in antiquity were a peripatetic class, though not a nomadic ethnic group. What the *qen-iy* "smith" (Kenite) was in the 'Arabah, the *Egene* was in Igbirra land in Nigeria.

# Notes

## Introduction

1. Cf. Edward Ullendorf, *The Semitic Languages of Ethiopia* (London: Taylor's, 1955).

2. J. H. Greenberg, *Languages of Africa* (The Hague: Mouton & Co., 1969), p. 28.

## Chapter 1

1. Hebrew *ṣɛlɛm, ṣal*$^{e}$*m-* is, however, cognate with Mwaghavul *čilem* and Pyem *šulum,* both meaning "shadow" in the sense of "spiritual guardian, guardian angel" (cf. *morphé theou* in Phil. 2:6).

2. See John Okparocha, *MBARI—Art as Sacrifice* (Ibadan, Nigeria: Daystar Press, 1976).

## Chapter 2

1. The *nš* in Semitic becomes *ny* in West Africa: Kasele *enyi* "man"; Igbo *onye* "person"; Hebrew *'on*$^{e}$*š-ey* "men of"; Yoruba *èǹy-àn/òǹy-àn* "human being."

2. From the same root as Amharic *gebre* "messenger" (man as ambassador, apostle, emissary of the gods).

3. There is no possibility of a white lion or a black lion. The lion establishes a connection between the tawny color and extreme vitality—power.

4. *Bruno* means "brown."

5. Aramaic *bar* "soil" also indicates this redness of the soil, for it is cognate with Igbo *ọbara* "blood" and with Hebrew *bar* "corn" (the reddish-colored varieties) and *'abiyr* "bull" (that embodiment of vitality and virile power). For how *Edom* got his name, see Gen. 25:29–30.

6. "The life of the animal is in its *dam*."

7. For this reason Africans recognized their oldest ancestor in a va-

riety of *ta-b*$^{e}$*n-iyt* "physical forms"—animals, trees, rocks; for the characteristic of an ancient ancestor is not in *ta-b*$^{e}$*n-iyt* but in *d*$^{e}$*m-u*$^{w}$*t*—life force, vitality. "Dinka totems are usually animal, sometimes plant, more rarely a natural object or process. . . . The clans speak of certain animals as their 'ancestors', *kwar*. . . . The clans are usually designated by the name of their traditional first human ancestor; comparatively few are spoken of by the name of their animal, though there is a Niel (snake) clan . . ." (C. G. Seligman, *Pagan Tribes of the Nilotic Sudan* [London: George Routledge & Sons, 1932], pp. 142–43). The cognomen (the third name) of Oyo Yoruba people usually reveals what their totemic ancestor is.

8. Note that in African belief the chief guardian of morality is Mother Earth.

9. Just as *'abiyr-iym* "strong beings" is rendered as "angels" in Ps. 78:25, the *'-b-r* root being from the same biconsonantal base as Igbo *ọbara* "blood," Grebo *bro* "farm," and Aramaic *bar* "field."

10. Roberto Pazzi, *L'homme—Eve, Aja, Gɛn, Fọn—et son univers,* vol. 1 (Lomé, Togo, 1976), p. 99.

11. See Philip Stevens, *The Soap Stone Images of Esie* (Ibadan, Nigeria: Ibadan University Press, 1979).

12. See Igbo *arúsi/alúsi* "divinities, divine ancestors."

13. Adam called his wife *Ḥawwah* "because she was the mother of all *ḥay*" (Gen. 3:20). For Hebrew *ḥay*, read Yoruba *Ẹ̀yọ̀*. For Hebrew *Ḥawwah*, read Jukun *wuwa* "woman," and Hausa *uwa* "mother."

14. See Field, *Search for Security* (London: Faber & Faber, 1960), p. 79.

15. The argument goes thus: *(i)* Since the Chadic languages (e.g., Hahm/Jaba) have been accepted as related to Semitic (e.g., Hebrew), cognate reflexes of Hebrew words may be found in Hahm/Jaba. *(ii)* Since the triconsonantal root in Semitic words is generally reflected as biconsonantal in "Hamitic" languages, Hebrew *Ḥano*$^{w}$*k* (*ḥ-n-k)* could be expected to reflect in "Hamitic" the word *Nok (n-k)*, the two strong consonants being retained. *(iii)* Now the name of the first city, according to Gen. 4:17, is *Ḥano*$^{w}$*k*; and the name of the first civilization (= city culture) in West Africa is the Nok culture, according to the present state of archeological studies. *(iv)* The city of *Ḥano*$^{w}$*k* was built by *Qayin* = smith; Nok in West Africa has yielded the earliest trace of iron working in West Africa: third century B.C. *(v)* Moreover, the people of *Nok* (the Hahm) attribute iron smelting to a mythical figure, *Kuno*, which I say is a reflex of mythical *Qayin*.

16. See Byang Kato, *Theological Pitfalls in Africa* (Kisumu, Kenya: Evangel Publishing House, 1975), pp. 27–28.

17. Ibid., p. 37. Note that in primal world-views iron is not the only metal that is considered to be a spirit. Gold is also considered to be a spirit. Hence both Twi and Gã *sika* "gold" (Hebrew *zakak* "be translucent"; *z*$^{e}$*kok-iyt* "glass": Yoruba *dígí, jígí* "mirror, glass") is reflected in Acholi as *jok* "spirit" (Ijọ *digi* "look at"; Egyptian *dgi* "look").

18. For the connection between the *qeyn-iy*, the peripatetic clan of smiths who were related to the father-in-law of Moses, see Judg. 1:16; 4:11; Num. 10:29; 24:21. Because he was peripatetic, the Genesis account says that their ancestor, *Qayin*, received a curse from God: "A fugitive and a wanderer shalt thou be. . . ."

## Chapter 3

1. See Modupẹ Oduyọye, "Anti-Hamitism in Genesis," in Jesse Mugambe, ed., *Racism in Theology and Theology against Racism* (Geneva: World Council of Churches, 1975).

2. Compare the consonantal roots *N-m-r-d/L-m-r-d.*

3. Francis Mading Deng, *The Dinka of the Sudan* (New York: Holt, Rinehart, and Winston, 1972), p. 1.

4. Ngas *go* "people": Mwaghavul *gu* "people": Luo *jo* "people": Hebrew *go*$^{w}$*y* "nation, people."

5. J. H. Greenberg, *Languages of Africa* (The Hague: Mouton & Co., 1969), p. 50. The more remote the linguistic relationship, the more the relevant corpus will be found embedded in mythology.

## Chapter 4

1. The Hebrew phrase *miq-qɛdɛm* seems to give an idea of the location/direction of *'Edɛn*. It is translated as "in the east" by the Revised Standard Version (R.S.V.) in Gen. 2:8. But the same phrase *miq-qɛdɛm* occurs in Hab. 1:12: *h*$^{a}$*-lo*$^{w}$*' 'attah miq-qɛdɛm YHWH* ("Are you not from *qɛdɛm*, Yahweh?"). Here the R.S.V., realizing that it does not make sense to ask Yahweh, "Are you not from the east?" says "Art thou not from everlasting?"

So Hebrew *qɛdɛm* can refer to time past (Hab. 1:12) or to direction "east." Why, then, cannot *qɛdɛm* in Gen. 2:8 be "the mythical past"?

> And *Yahweh '*$^{ɛ}$*loh-iym* planted a *gan* from everlasting.
>
> And Yahweh *'*$^{ɛ}$*loh-iym* planted a *gan* in the mythical past.

Why not?

2. Having accounted for the interrupted progress of nomadism by

positing *Hɛbɛl*'s murder by the farmer-technologist, urban-dwelling line of *Qayin*, the Hebrews, who contributed practically nothing to ancient science, technology, urbanization, or civilization, banished *Qayin* into the land of Nod (restlessness). This explains why the Hebrew Scriptures is not a book about science or technology or civilization. By Gen. 4:24 the Hebrew writers had closed the book on the fortunes of the family of *Qayin*. With the announcement in Gen. 4:25 that "Adam knew his wife again . . ." the Hebrews turned their faces toward the area of culture in which they shone brilliantly: religion.

In closing the page on the *to$^{w}$-l$^{e}$d-o$^{w}$t* of *Qayin*, the Hebrew writers blacked out the history of civilization in Africa (see Wọlé Ṣoyinka, *Ògún Abibiman*). It must be remembered that the Hebrews wrote their Scriptures after they had escaped from the pyramid-building civilization of Egypt. Pharaonic Egypt began in 3100 B.C.; the Hyksos did not invade Egypt until about 1785 B.C.. They were expelled in 1550 B.C. and the civilization of the Pharaohs continued its own destiny until Cleopatra's death in 31 B.C. Israel got its first king about 1025 B.C.

## Chapter 5

1. W. B. Anderson, *The Church in East Africa, 1840–1974* (Dodoma, Tanzania: Central Tanganyika Press, 1977), p. 55.

2. Ibid., p. 22.

3. The phonological correspondence is Semitic *'l-h:* Yoruba *-l-w-* when the thematic vowel is a back vowel: Hebrew *'$^{ɛ}$loah:* Yoruba *olúwa* "lord," *Olúwo* "leader of the *Ọ̀ṣùgbó* council"; *orúwo* "head."

4. Gerhard von Rad says, "Every word of this little sentence is difficult: . . . The passage can no longer be clarified" (*Genesis* [London: SCM Press, 1961], p. 100). In the context of Ewe world-view, there is no difficulty in a statement which says that *Gún* is a *Yɛhwe,* for they use *Yɛhwe* as Seth used it in Gen. 4:26, long before Moses. "Chez les Eve occidentaux, le nom 'Vodu' est generalement remplacé par 'Trõ' . . . et par 'Yèvè' (cf. Esprit, N.B. I) s'il s'agit de la Foudre" (Roberto Pazzi, *L'homme—Eve, Aja, Gɛn, Fọn—et son univers*, vol. 1 [Lomé, Togo: 1976], p. 302).

5. Robert H. Pfeiffer, *Religion in the Old Testament* (New York: Harper & Brothers, 1961), pp. 40–41.

6. Efik *ẹnyọn* "uppermost," a title of God in the Efik name *Ekpeyong* "priest of the Most High," is paralleled in Hebrew usage: *Mal$^{e}$k-iy ṣɛdɛq* (Gen. 14:18–20) was an *Ekpeyong*.

7. Pazzi, *L'homme—Eve, Aja, Gɛn, Fọn—et son univers*, p. 295.

8. See Modupẹ Oduyọye, *The Promised Land* (Ibadan, Nigeria: Daystar Press, 1979), pp. 50–51, n. 1.

## Chapter 6

1. Hebrew *mab-bu$^{w}$l* (Gen. 7:17a): Chichewa *m-vula:* Bemba *m-fula:* Se-tswana *pula* "rain." "An understanding of the Priestly story of the flood depends materially on the correct translation of the word *mabbūl. Mabbūl* does not mean 'flood' " (Gerhard von Rad, *Genesis* [London: SCM Press, 1961], p. 124).

2. See Modupẹ Oduyọye, "Mr. John Ricketts," in *The Nigerian Christian* 9, no. 7 (1975): 2. John Ricketts ran passenger boats from Ikorodu to Lagos, Nigeria, for many years before the construction of the Lagos to Ikorodu Road.

3. For the connection in the mind of ancient people between the dazzle of the rainbow, the dazzle of the skin of serpents, the dazzle of gold (and other precious metals), and permanent exemption from destruction (from penury or from flood), see Hebrew *nahaš* "serpent" (in Eden); *n$^{e}$hoš-εt* "copper, bronze"; *n$^{e}$ḥaš n$^{e}$ḥuš-$^{e}$t-an* "serpent of bronze" (which Moses hoisted up on a pole in the wilderness to save the Israelites from death [Num. 21:9] and which was worshiped by the Israelites later [2 Kings 18:4]). For a version of the myth of the rainbow as a python, see John Okparocha, *MBARI—Art as Sacrifice* (Ibadan, Nigeria: Daystar Press, 1976), pp. 44–49.

4. Folk etymology is the lay explanation for the origin of words. Frequently folk explanation differs from the origin of the word as explained by philologists.

5. The *nwḥ* root in *Noaḥ* is reflected in Shona as *nhu:*

| | |
|---|---|
| *u-nhu* | "the correct way of living, good character" |
| *mu-nhu* | "a person who has good character and morality" |

"A person who steals, is rude or of bad character is said to be poorly endowed with *unhu* and this . . . is traced back to his parents or even further . . ." (Michael Gelfand, *The Genuine Shona* [Gwelo, Zimbabwe: Mambo Press, 1973], p. 140).

## Chapter 7

1. See Ps. 103:16:

*kiy ru$^{w}$aḥ 'ab$^{e}$r-ah b-o$^{w}$*
*w$^{e}$-'eyn-εy-nu$^{w}$;*
*w$^{e}$-lo' yak-kiyr-εn-nu$^{w}$ 'o$^{w}$d m$^{e}$-qo$^{w}$m-o$^{w}$.*

The wind blows over him
  and he disappears;
And the place where he was can no longer be recognized.

Hebrew *suʷfah* "gale" is Yoruba *súfèé* "whistle," Chichewa *chi sumphi* "the god of the storm."

2. Ibid.

3. See Roland de Vaux, *The Early History of Israel* (London: Darton, Longman & Todd, 1978), p. 222.

4. Ibid., p. 229.

5. Albright, *From the Stone Age to Christianity* (Garden City, N.Y.: Doubleday Anchor Books, 1957), p. 63.

6. Ibid., p. 44.

7. Ibid., p. 240, n. 54.

8. Derrick S. Stenning, *Savannah Nomads* (London: International African Institute/Oxford University Press, 1959), p. 104.

9. Ibid.

10. Quoted in B. A. Ogot, *Zamani* (Nairobi: East African Publishing House, 1968), p. 94.

11. Dennis Williams, "African Iron and the Classical World," in *Africa in Classical Antiquity* (Ibadan: Ibadan University Press, 1969), p. 79.

12. Gerhard von Rad, *Genesis* (London: SCM Press, 1961), p. 104.

13. See Modupẹ Oduyọye, *Yoruba Names—Their Structure and Their Meanings* (Ibadan, Nigeria: Daystar Press, 1972).

14. Michael A. Hoffman, *Egypt before the Pharaohs* (London: Routledge & Kegan Paul, 1980), p. 242.

15. Ibid., pp. 241–42.

16. Ibid., p. 207.

17. Ibid., p. 205.

18. *Ebira,* the real name of the farming people whom others call Igbirra, is comparable to the name of *Hɛbɛr* in Judg. 4:11, 17. He is called *haq-qeyn-iy* "the Kenite," which is to say that the Ebira people are of the same ancestry as the *Egene* caste of smiths who live in the same part of Nigeria with them. *Hɛbɛr* had cut himself off from the tribe of *Qayin* and the clan of the sons of Hobab, the father-in-law of Moses!

## Chapter 8

1. G. Johannes Botterweck and Helmer Ringgren, eds., *Theological Dictionary of the Old Testament*, vol. 1 (Grand Rapids, Mich.: Wm. B. Eerdmans, 1977 rev. ed.), p. 467.

## Epilogue

1. Refer to the theological controversy created by the Arians, who understood Jesus as *homoíōsis* of God—a likeness of God. The view that Jesus was *homoousios*—of the same essence—with God prevailed.

2. M. J. Field, *Search for Security: An Ethno-Psychiatric Study of Rural Ghana* (London: Faber & Faber, 1960), pp. 112–13.

3. W. Neil, *One Volume Bible Commentary* (London: Hodder & Stoughton, 1962), p. 16. See also J. Y. Campbell, "Image," in Alan Richardson, ed., *A Theological Dictionary of the Bible* (London: SCM Press, 1950).

4. "Amongst Chevieso's cult objects are . . . the so-called So-stones, alleged to have arrived with the lightning, as well as a two-edged axe forged out of iron, . . . the lightning axe. Chevieso is the most important guardian spirit of the so-called Yehwe cult groups. . . . Professor Herskovits . . . maintains that in Dahomey the name Yehwe is a synonym of vodu; both mean divine" (H. Debrunner, *A Church between Colonial Powers: A Study of the Church in Togo* [London: Lutterworth Press, 1965], p. 58). See Herskovits, *Dahomey*, vol. II, pp. 190–94. Also Spieth, *Die Religion der Eweer*, p. iii.

5. Arthur Markowitz, *The Rebirth of the Ostrich* (Gaberone, Botswana: National Museum and Art Gallery, 1971), p. 74.

6. Thomas Berry, "The Indian Future," *Cross Currents* 26, no. 2 (Summer 1976): 139.

## Appendix

1. M. E. L. Mallowan, "Nimrud," in D. Winton Thomas, ed., *Archaeology and Old Testament Study*, Jubilee Volume of the [British] Society for Old Testament Study 1917–1967 (Oxford: Clarendon Press, 1967).

2. E. A. Speiser, *Genesis* (Garden City, N.Y.: Doubleday & Co., 1964), p. 66.

3. Ibid., p. 20.

4. A. N. Tucker, "What's in a Name?" in Bynon and Bynon, eds., *Hamito-Semitica* (The Hague: Mouton, 1974).

5. J. H. Greenberg, "Language, Diffusion and Migration," in Anwar S. Dil, ed., *Language, Culture and Communication* (Stanford, Calif.: Stanford University Press, 1971), p. 93.

6. Edward Ullendorf, *Ethiopia and the Bible* (London: Taylor's, 1955), pp. 3-4.

7. B. S. J. Isserling, "Some Aspects of the Present State of Hamito-Semitic Studies," in Bynon and Bynon, eds., *Hamito-Semitica*, p.3.

8. Samuel Johnson, *The History of the Yorubas* (Lagos, Nigeria: CMS Bookshops, 1921), pp. 5-6.

9. Ibid., pp. 3-7.

10. Herman Gunkel, *The Legends of Genesis* (New York: Schocken Books, 1964), p. 90.

11. Ibid., p. 159.

12. Roberto Pazzi, *L'homme—Eve, Aja, Gɛn, Fọn—et son univers*, vol. 1 (Lomé, Togo, 1976), p. 295.

13. Robert H. Pfeiffer, *Religion in the Old Testament* (New York: Harper & Row, 1961), pp. 52-53.

14. See H. Debrunner, *A Church between Colonial Powers*, p. 58.

15. E. A. Speiser, *Genesis*, pp. 61-62.

16. John B. Thompson, "On the Interpretation of Language and Ideology," *Media Development* 30, no. 1 (London, 1983): 14.

17. *Encyclopaedia Judaica* 5 (Jerusalem, 1971): 97-98.

18. See John Roscoe, *The Baganda* (London: Macmillan and Co., 1911).

19. *Encyclopaedia Judaica*, pp. 97-98.

20. Norman Gottwald, *A Light to the Nations* (New York: Harper & Row, 1959), p. 540.

21. Ibid., p. 544.

22. Ibid., p. 545; cf. pp. 91, 162.

23. Roland de Vaux, *The Early History of Israel* (London: Darton, Longman & Todd, 1978), p. 214.

24. Siegfried Herrmann, *Israel in Egypt* (London: SCM Press, 1973), p. 34 (to be read in context of pp. 33-37).

25. George V. Pixley, *God's Kingdom* (Maryknoll, N.Y.: Orbis Books, 1981), p. 30.

26. Roman Jakobson, *Main Trends in the Science of Language* (London: George Allen & Unwin, 1973), p. 40.

27. Roland de Vaux, *The Early History of Israel*, pp. 106-12, 209-15; quotation from pp. 110-11.

28. J. B. Callender, "Grammatical Models in Egyptology," in Giorgio Buccellati, ed., *Approaches to the Study of the Ancient Near East* (Los Angeles: Undena Publications, 1973), p. 73.

29. Roland de Vaux, *The Early History of Israel*, p. 213.

30. E. A. Speiser, *Genesis*, p. 31.

31. Carleton Hodge, ed., *Afroasiatic—A Survey* (The Hague: Mouton, 1971), p. 6.

32. See Graham Connah, "The Coming of Iron: Nok and Daima," in Thurston Shaw, ed., *Lectures on Nigerian Prehistory and Archaeology* (Ibadan: Ibadan University Press, 1969).

# Indexes

## Index of Hebrew and Related Semitic Words (Akkadian, Arabic, Aramaic, Assyrian, Babylonian, Syriac, Ugaritic)

*(Words from African Semitic languages appear in the Index of African Words)*


*‘aalam*, cosmos (Arabic), 48
*‘abar*, cross over, trespass, pass on, pass by, 63, 64
*’abiyr*, bull, 108n5
*’abiyr-iym*, strong beings, 109n9
*‘abo$^w$r su$^w$fah*, wind whistling by, 63, 68, 69
*’adam, ha-’adam*, ancestral man, 5, 6, 7, 8, 12, 13, 15-19, 20, 24, 25, 33, 39, 40, 47, 69, 75, 81, 85, 86, 87, 88, 104
*’adam-ah, ha-’adam-ah*, (top)soil, red soil, 7, 8, 9, 13, 16, 17, 20, 21, 41, 87
*’adam y$^e$lu$^w$d ’iššah*, man (*’adam*) born of woman, 16, 17, 88
*’ah*, brother, 85
*’aḥ-iy’el* (Ahiel), genius, 84, 85, 86
*-ah* suffix, 9
*‘Akkad* (Accad), 27, 93
*‘alam*, conceal, 48
*’Al-baari*, the fashioner (title of God) (Arabic), 11
*’al-bariy’*, creator (God) (Arabic), 18
*’al jannah*, see *jannah*
*’allu$^w$f*, ruler, chief, beloved, 11
*’amar*, to say, 11
*’amar*, to command (Arabic), 11
*’amiyr*, ruler (emir, admiral, commander) (Arabic), 11
*’anaš-iym* (masc. pl. of *’$^e$no$^w$š*, q.v.), 16, 52
*’an$^e$š-ey haš-šem*, renowned human beings, 31
*‘apar, ‘ap$^e$r-o$^w$t*, dust, 7, 9, 13, 67
*‘Apiru* (*Habiru*, Accadian; *Hapiru*, Ugaritic), 66–67, 101–104
*‘apr-m*, nomads, 103; see also *‘prm*
*’arak*, to be long, 18
*‘ar$^e$m-ah*, craftiness, 48

## Index of African Words

-*wa* suffix (Hausa), 67
*w3g*, religious festival (Egyptian), 72
*wúrà*, gold (Yoruba), 106
*wuwa*, woman (Jukun), 104, 109n13
*yè*, to survive, to live through (Yoruba), 105
*Yɛhwe*, spirit, divine spirit (Fọn), 20, 32, 50, 51, 52, 87, 97, 98, 111n4, 114n4
*Yèvè*, spirit (Ewe), 50, 52, 97, 98, 111n4
*Yihwe Yɛhwe*, God (Gun), 50
*yíóò kú*, he will die (Yoruba), 106
*Yorùbá*, land toward the sunset, 28
*zákì*, lion (Hausa), 106


## Index of Consonantal Roots



## Index of Scriptural References